MEDLINE

A Guide to
Effective Searching in
PubMed and Other Interfaces

Second Edition

Brian S. Katcher

THE ASHBURY PRESS
SAN FRANCISCO
2006

The Ashbury Press
San Francisco, CA
www.ashburypress.com

The following names are trademarks of the National
Library of Medicine®: *Index Medicus*®, Loansome Doc®,
MEDLARS®, MEDLINE®, MedlinePlus®, MeSH®,
Metathesaurus®, NLM®, PubMed®, PubMed Central®,
UMLS®, Unified Medical Language System®, and
Visible Human Project®.

The quotation from Shunryu Suzuki's *Zen Mind,
Beginner's Mind* on page vi is copyright 1970 by John
Weatherhill, Inc. and is used with permission.

The abstract from the *New England Journal of Medicine*
on page 25 is copyright 2004, Massachusetts Medical
Society and used with permission.

The quotation of John Shaw Billings on page 45 is
copyright 1965, the Medical Library Association and is
used with permission.

The quotation on pages 81–82 is copyright 1997
Epidemiology and is used with permission.

Although great care was taken in the preparation of
this book, no warranty can be made with regard to
its contents, or its application. The user of MEDLINE/
PubMed assumes responsibility for his or her own
searches. Consumers of health care should use
MedlinePlus and consult with health professionals.

Library of Congress Control Number: 2005911335
ISBN 13: 978-0-9673445-1-5
ISBN 10: 0-9673445-1-4

To Betty and Sonya

If a man will begin with certainties,
he shall end in doubts,
but if he will be content to begin with doubts,
he shall end in certainties.

Francis Bacon ~ *The Advancement of Learning (1605)*

In the beginner's mind
there are many possibilities,
but in the expert's there are few.

Shunru Suzuki ~ *Zen Mind, Beginner's Mind (1970)*

Preface

I am extremely grateful to have had the opportunity to create this thoroughly revised second edition. Like its predecessor, it is intended to be read from start to finish, away from the computer. This book is not intended as a replacement for the excellent MEDLINE tutorials on the Web (see Appendix A), the classes that are offered by most medical libraries, or the on-line help that comes with PubMed, Ovid, and other interfaces to MEDLINE. PubMed's on-line tutorial is an especially good complement to this book, which has a more ambitious agenda—the cultivation of an informed and thoughtful approach to searching in MEDLINE.

The search examples in this book reflect my two main interests: the clinical use of drugs for common health problems and public health strategies to reduce the burden of these problems. They are only examples, selected to illustrate how MEDLINE works. I am painfully aware of how quickly a book like this becomes dated and have attempted to place time-sensitive information in Appendix A, which is also on the Web (www.ashburypress.com/medline/resources). As in the past, the Web version will be periodically updated. MEDLINE is but one of many tools for learning about biomedical knowledge, so this edition's Appendix A has been expanded to include a section on sources of health information on the Web. It is but a small sampling; suggestions are welcomed! As previously, Medical Subject Headings appear as SMALL CAPS.

MEDLINE's basic features have changed somewhat in the half-dozen years since the publication of the first edition, but to a large extent it is the same remarkable bibliographic database that it has always been. More significant changes have occurred (and will no doubt continue to occur) in its most widely used interface,

PubMed. PubMed provides access to citations in MEDLINE (the primary component of PubMed), to citations from journals that are outside of MEDLINE's scope, to citations that are in the process of being indexed for MEDLINE, and to citations that were indexed before MEDLINE's existence. PubMed's other features, including its capacity for linkages to other Web-based resources and its capacity for mapping entry terms to MEDLINE data elements, are described in Chapters 1 and 2. More information on the difference between MEDLINE and PubMed can be found on a National Library of Medicine Fact Sheet (see page 100).

PubMed has made it easier to search in MEDLINE. Nevertheless, the popularization of powerful Web search engines like Google has changed our standards for finding information. Our expectations are higher, and our patience is lower. We are accustomed to using Google for queries that take far less than a minute. MEDLINE can be fast, but it is a different beast. Effective searches require a little planning, and refinement as well. The Web is completely unorganized; MEDLINE is elegantly organized. Google takes us first to the most widely cited and frequently used sources that match our query. MEDLINE places no premium on the popularity of its citations; it expects us to ask carefully, unambiguously—and it provides the means for doing so.

My first experience with MEDLINE was in 1971. I was a young clinical pharmacist and assistant professor at the University of California, San Francisco (UCSF) School of Pharmacy. As a member of the Library Committee, I was among the first to learn that the National Library of Medicine was offering free MEDLINE searches for faculty. My query—a broad request for citations concerning drug therapy for arthritis—produced a printout on fan-folded paper that was approximately twelve inches high. It was too large to be helpful, but I was impressed by the resources that had been used to produce it. The printout sat in my office for many years, serving as a kind of totem. Over the years, I edited several editions of a multi-authored textbook on the clinical use of drugs, using the printed *Index Medicus* as my guide to journal articles. Then, in 1983, I bought my first personal computer, and, with it, a 1200 baud modem (fast for that era). I subscribed to an evening version of Dialog, which provided MEDLINE access for $48 per hour, half the daytime rate. Eventually, I took a several-day course provided by the National Library of Medicine (NLM) at UCLA. With the help of several binders and reference books produced by the NLM, and an excellent book on command-line MEDLINE searching (the late Susan Feinglos's *MEDLINE: A Basic Guide to Searching*, 1985), my search skills improved. The training course allowed subsequent access to a now-defunct MEDLINE server at the NLM for a much lower connect rate. My many searches were enormously valuable in writing a book for older users of prescription drugs, published in 1988. By the 1990s, I had free access to MEDLINE through a dial-up connection to the library at UCSF (and by then my modem was faster). MEDLINE was my constant support in a career transition to public health. During a postdoctoral fellowship in alcohol research at the University of California, Berkeley School of Public Health, MEDLINE was one of my main tools. Inspired by the usefulness of my experiences, I resolved to write a book about MEDLINE itself, independent of any specific interface. This objective was realized with the publication of the first edition of this book, in 1999. That was two years after the launch of PubMed, which introduced free MEDLINE on the Web.

I am indebted to my colleagues at the San Francisco Department of Public Health, who graciously supported the part-time schedule that allowed me to work on this project, to medical librarians and colleagues who read drafts of this and the previous edition, to the NLM, and to my family. Judith Bishop, Michael Delander, Jan Glover, Mary Keane, Bob Liner, Kelly Near, David Owen, Jessica Warner, and my wife Betty provided many helpful suggestions. Any faults are my own.

Contents

Introduction

WHEN you open PubMed, the most widely used interface to MEDLINE, you are greeted with a query box. It looks like Google's, but the query boxes of PubMed and Google are portals into vastly different worlds. Google brings you to the World Wide Web, a huge and amorphous mass of documents that are connected by links. It analyzes those links to impose order on the Web. MEDLINE, on the other hand, is an exquisitely organized bibliographic database. PubMed makes extensive use of MEDLINE's organization in translating our queries.

MEDLINE is the collective product of a small army of indexers, who have, for more than 40 years, systematically characterized the contents of more than 4,800 journals that publish information about the causes, prevention, and treatment of disease and injury. Each of the more than thirteen million journal articles, letters, and editorials that are catalogued in MEDLINE has been read by a skilled indexer, who has assigned to it roughly a dozen Medical Subject Headings, drawn from a controlled vocabulary of more than 23,000 such terms (MeSH terms). These MeSH terms, which describe concepts, are sometimes qualified with subheadings. Additional concepts are indexed in Supplementary Concept Records, and the articles themselves are characterized as to their Publication Type. This manual indexing (and disambiguation), which augments an extensive system of automated indexing, is applied with a high degree of consistency. If you understand the elaborate indexing schemes that are embodied in MEDLINE, you can use this understanding to search it with a high degree of precision.

If you have not had much experience with MEDLINE, this might be a good time to look at the Web-based MEDLINE tutorials described in Appendix A. This book will teach you how to use MEDLINE, but tutorials (and classes) will speed the process and will facilitate this book's main mission, teaching you to think critically in applying MEDLINE's power.

Size is also important. Because its coverage is so broad, MEDLINE can be thought of as the index to the world's medical literature, the on-line catalogue of biomedical journal articles. It is an essential tool for assessing the scientific basis for current knowledge about health. MEDLINE is produced by the National Library of Medicine and is the largest and best organized database of its kind. But MEDLINE searching can be daunting, producing results that are too comprehensive or too limited to be useful, hence this book.

The story of MEDLINE's origins and evolution, which sets the stage for understanding how this powerful database works, is told in Chapter 1. Chapter 2 describes the key indexing elements that are used to characterize articles in MEDLINE. This chapter also begins to show how this indexing information can be used to find articles, using the PubMed interface to MEDLINE as an example. Because Medical Subject Headings (MeSH terms) are so important to searching in MEDLINE, they are described in greater depth in Chapter 3. (Throughout the text, MeSH terms are set in SMALL CAPITAL LETTERS.) Chapter 4 illustrates how Publication Types can be used to focus a search, and Chapter 5 contains some practical tips.

There is no single, perfect way to search in MEDLINE. This book is designed to help you search with an understanding of what is possible and not be disappointed.

1
Origins of MEDLINE and Why It Works the Way It Does

FIRST, consider how MEDLINE came to be created, and how it evolved. This will give you the basis for understanding how it works.

Origins

In 1864, toward the end of the Civil War, John Shaw Billings, a 27-year-old military surgeon, was transferred from field duty to the Surgeon General's Office in Washington. His new assignment included, among other things, care of the modest collection of books and journals that was the Surgeon General's Library. During the years that followed, Billings aggressively expanded the collection, building it into the country's largest medical library. In 1876, he told the Surgeon General that it "may now be properly called the National Medical Library" (Garrison 1915) — a name that, by the middle of the twentieth century, would become the "National Library of Medicine."

Billings then developed an elaborate system for cataloguing everything within the Library. At the time, most libraries did not attempt to catalogue their books by subject, though the practice was beginning to be introduced. Users were accustomed to locating books by author and then searching the indexes of individual books to find information about a particular topic. In one of his first bold innovations, Billings designed a cataloguing system that included both subjects and author names in his *Index Catalogue of the Library of the Surgeon General's Office* (NLM 2004). Because the Library's collection was so extensive, its well-indexed *Catalogue,* which was printed as a multi-volume series, came to be regarded as an index to the world's medical literature (Garrison 1915).

This was the era in which articles in medical journals were beginning to challenge books as the primary means for disseminating medical knowledge, and Billings included medical journal articles within this huge index of the Library's holdings. However, the publication of medical journal articles occurred much faster than the indexing process for the entire Library. To keep up with this growing medical periodical literature, Billings created the *Index Medicus,* an index to articles published in medical journals. Beginning in 1879, the *Index Medicus* was published monthly and cumulated annually. From this point forward, the Library took on the task of characterizing and indexing the world's periodical medical literature. As Billings described it in Vol. 1, No. 1,

> The *Index Medicus* will record the titles of all new publications in Medicine, Surgery, and the collateral branches, received during the preceding month. These will be classed under subject headings, and these will be followed by the titles of valuable original articles upon the same subject, found, during the like period, in medical journals and transactions of medical societies. The periodicals thus indexed will comprise all current medical journals and transactions of value, so far as they can be obtained (Billings 1879).

These subject headings evolved steadily over the years, and the number of indexed journal articles increased, but the greatest changes occurred during the 1960s, when the *Index Medicus* was modified so that it could be published simultaneously as a printed publication and as a computerized database.

From Punch Cards to Computers

The computerization of the *Index Medicus,* which ultimately led to MEDLINE, drew upon another innovation from John Shaw Billings's extraordinary career (he also designed the Johns Hopkins Hospital, shaped the curriculum of the Johns Hopkins Medical School, recruited William Osler for its faculty, and presided over the development of the New York Public Library system). Billings's interest in public health and vital statistics led to work on the U.S. Census. Seeking a way to improve the organization of data for the Census, he suggested storing information as punched holes on a card, so that the cards could later be sorted according to the alignment of the holes that had been punched in them. As Billings described it, the various statistical data "might be recorded on a single card or slip by punching holes in it, and…these cards might then be assorted and counted by mechanical means according to any selected group of these perforations" (Garrison 1915). The recipient of this suggestion was Herman Hollerith, a young engineer who was working on the eleventh (1890) Census. Hollerith perfected the cards and developed a machine for sorting them. The cards subsequently became known as "Hollerith cards," though Hollerith never disputed that the original idea was Billings's. In 1896, Hollerith disseminated this technology to the general public by setting up the Tabulating Machine Company, which eventually was absorbed into a corporation called International Business Machines, or IBM. By the 1960s, Hollerith cards—IBM punch cards—would be made with punch holes corresponding to the Medical Subject Headings (MeSH) in the *Index Medicus* (Garrison 1915; Cummings 1966; Chapman 1987).

The relevance of IBM cards to the computerization of the *Index Medicus* becomes apparent when we look at the history of the science of information retrieval. After World War II, research in many scientific fields—including the biomedical sciences—began to explode. To keep up with the resulting flood of new journal articles, the science of information retrieval was born. A 1963 Air Force research report noted that human knowledge was increasing at an unprecedented rate, with more scientific research seeming to have been done in the preceding 20 years than in the 200 years before those busy decades (Barnard and Abbott 1963). This same report characterized the work of organizing this flood of knowledge as follows:

> The effort to bring this means up to an atomic-age standard is the science of information retrieval. As a recognizable, distinct science, it is no more than 15 years old [i.e., since 1948], but it now absorbs about one-eighth of the nation's research and development budget. Although libraries and classification systems since the time of Aristotle have performed the function of identifying the location of a specific bit of information, conventional systems are inadequate under the massive burden of recent years. Since World War II, a great amount of study has been applied to the development of the most logical and foolproof methods of indexing materials. With the development of electronic computers, much attention has been given to the mechanics of storage and retrieval (Barnard and Abbott 1963).

Punch Cards and Boolean Searching

The computers of the 1950s and 1960s relied on punch cards to carry out their information-processing tasks. Although the cumbersome sorting of punch cards has long-since been replaced by manipulations that take place almost instantaneously within computer memory, the essential process is the same. Therefore, the sorting of punch cards is a useful way to understand the inner workings of a computer database such as MEDLINE.

The single most important task that is accomplished by the sorting of punch cards is finding information by identifying the intersection of two or more index terms. Here is an example. In a printed index, such as the *Index Medicus,* if one were looking for information on the treatment of OSTEOARTHRITIS with the drug IBUPROFEN (to use a post-1960s example), one would look through all the listings under the Medical Subject Heading IBUPROFEN, scanning for entries concerning its use in OSTEOARTHRITIS—ignoring entries concerning its use in FEVER, reports of DRUG INTERACTIONS between IBUPROFEN and other drugs, rare cases of IBUPROFEN-induced kidney problems (KIDNEY FAILURE, ACUTE), etc. As an alternate approach, one could look under the Medical

Subject Heading OSTEOARTHRITIS and scan all of its entries, looking for those concerning its drug therapy with IBUPROFEN—and ignoring all others (ignoring, for example, articles about the use of ASPIRIN or NAPROXEN in OSTEOARTHRITIS, the HEALTH CARE COSTS of OSTEOARTHRITIS, etc). If punch cards were being used, this narrowing process would take place automatically. All the cards would be machine sorted to find those with a punch hole corresponding to IBUPROFEN. These IBUPROFEN cards would then be re-sorted to find those with a punch hole corresponding to OSTEOARTHRITIS. The resulting cards, dealing with both IBUPROFEN AND OSTEOARTHRITIS, would be of greatest use to the person who initiated the search.

AND. This successive sorting, first with one index term and then with another, to find entries that are indexed under *both* terms, is an example of the Boolean "AND." The descriptive term "Boolean" is named after George Boole, the nineteenth century mathematician who first described this system of logic. Careful use of the Boolean "AND" (always in upper case) is essential to effective searching in MEDLINE. Some probable relationships among the Medical Subject Headings mentioned in the previous paragraph are illustrated in Table 1-1 (page 8), which depicts the intersection of IBUPROFEN AND OSTEOARTHRITIS with a check mark. The Boolean "AND" is illustrated graphically in Figure 1-1 (page 9).

OR. Another form of Boolean logic is "OR," which can be thought of as meaning "either...or." For example, if one were interested in the treatment of OSTEOARTHRITIS with either ASPIRIN OR IBUPROFEN, all the cards in the system would be machine sorted to find those with a punch hole corresponding to ASPIRIN. These would be put aside. The remaining cards would again be sorted, this time looking for those with a punch hole corresponding to IBUPROFEN. These IBUPROFEN cards would be added to the stack of ASPIRIN cards. The resulting stack of cards indexed under ASPIRIN OR IBUPROFEN would then be sorted to find those with a punch hole corresponding to OSTEOARTHRITIS. The result of this (ASPIRIN OR IBUPROFEN) AND OSTEOARTHRITIS search would

TABLE 1-1
The Boolean "AND"

The result of a Boolean search for IBUPROFEN AND OSTEOARTHRITIS, as described on page 7, is shown with a check mark. Though this search was done with punch cards, the process would be fundamentally the same if it had taken place within computer memory.

The intersection of any of the Medical Subject Headings shown here describes an area of knowledge. For example, HEALTH CARE COSTS AND DRUG INTERACTIONS is another specific area of knowledge. Similarly, IBUPROFEN AND KIDNEY FAILURE, ACUTE is yet another area of knowledge. There is probably a literature at each of the intersection points in this table.[1]

	FEVER	OSTEO-ARTHRITIS	DRUG INTER-ACTIONS	KIDNEY FAILURE, ACUTE
ASPIRIN				
IBUPROFEN		✓		
NAPROXEN				
HEALTH CARE COSTS				

1. The full array of possible relationships of *all* Medical Subject Headings to all others might be imagined as a table with more than 23,000 rows and more than 23,000 columns. Of course, many of these possible intersection points would be empty of any literature. This kind of knowledge organization is best managed by a computer.

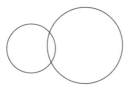

Figure 1-1. Graphic Depiction of the Boolean "AND." The circle on the left repre-sents all the journal articles indexed under IBUPROFEN. The circle on the right represents all the articles indexed under OSTEOARTHRITIS. Their overlap—the Boolean "AND"—represents articles indexed under both terms. Not drawn to scale.

be a specific stack of cards, each of which represented a journal publication concerning the treatment of OSTEOARTHRITIS with either ASPIRIN OR IBUPROFEN. As demonstrated by this example, the broadening strategy accomplished with the Boolean "OR" is usually followed by a narrowing strategy with the Boolean "AND." Another example would be (HYPOKALEMIA OR POTASSIUM) AND DIURETICS.

NOT. The third form of Boolean logic, "NOT," narrows the results of a search by excluding a specific index term. For example, if a search produced a stack of cards that was too large to be useful, they might be sorted to remove those cards that had a punch hole corresponding to the publication type "letter," thereby excluding letters to the editor from the search results. This type of Boolean logic must be applied with caution, because it can throw out use-ful material. For example, if you were interested in the clinical use of a drug, it might seem reasonable to exclude animal studies, but such a strategy—"NOT ANIMALS"—would exclude papers about the use of the drug in humans that begin with a discussion of ani-mal research. Generally speaking, "AND" is a better way to limit results. For example, "AND HUMANS" would eliminate papers that focus only on animals, without excluding those that deal with both humans and animals.

During the 1950s, the problems of categorization of subject

headings received intensive study, and a new system of Medical Subject Headings and standardized subheadings was designed to promote a clearer organization of concepts. At the time, IBM and other punch cards were the standard means by which information systems were operated, so the problems of using punch cards and their supporting apparatus of sorters also received careful study (Whittock and Larkey 1955).

Computerization of the *Index Medicus*

When a new system for production of the *Index Medicus* was put into operation in 1960, the National Library of Medicine hoped to achieve two objectives. The first was the creation of an automated system for mechanical production of the *Index Medicus* that would streamline its preparation for printing. The second objective was the application of coordinate indexing, which would allow Boolean searching, so that tailor-made bibliographic lists could be produced in response to specific questions. The system was successful in its first objective, using IBM punch cards to prepare the *Index Medicus*. However, the large number of cards proved too awkward to sort for Boolean searches in response to specific questions. The system was therefore redesigned, making information retrieval its primary objective (Rogers 1982).

The new and thoroughly revised list of Medical Subject Headings that had been introduced with the 1960 *Index Medicus* was completely redesigned in 1963. Many new headings were added, reflecting the frequency of appearance of specific subjects (concepts) that were previously indexed under broader concepts. For instance, DIABETES MELLITUS was combined with other concepts to produce new headings such as DIABETIC ANGIOPATHIES and DIABETIC NEU-ROPATHIES. The expanded list was divided into broad categories, such as Anatomical Terms, Organisms, Diseases, Chemicals and Drugs, etc. Terms were arranged hierarchically within these broad categories. The creation of this controlled vocabulary of Medical Subject Headings (MeSH), a powerful means for cataloging and retrieving articles (and books), was a major landmark in the history of biomedicine (Coletti and Bleich 2001; Sewell 1964).

The redesigned system, which was called the Medical Literature Analysis and Retrieval System (MEDLARS), ran on a computer that was programmed with magnetic tape. At the time, the printed output from computers was limited to a single font in upper case characters, but a new form of computer-driven photo-typesetting, capable of upper and lower case and multiple fonts and sizes, was specially developed to create the camera-ready pages for the 1964 *Index Medicus.* This new equipment pioneered computerized typesetting. At the same time, MEDLARS began functioning as an information retrieval system. The searches were slow—it took two and a half hours to read a magnetic tape file of a million citations. Nevertheless, the National Library of Medicine was running more than a thousand searches per month by the end of the 1960s. In 1971, the original magnetic tape-based MEDLARS system was converted to a faster on-line system: MEDLars on-LINE (MEDLINE) (Miles 1982; Rogers 1982).

The number of various subject headings that can be used to characterize an article must be sharply limited in a printed index. Otherwise, the number of pages in the index would become un-wieldy. In an electronic database, however, such physical limitations no longer exist, allowing an indexing scheme of far greater richness, which is what was developed for MEDLARS and MEDLINE. Instead of indexing a journal article under a mere two or three Medical Subject Headings, a dozen or more could be applied, along with additional subheadings or qualifiers. This density of indexing allows precisely focused searching in MEDLINE, but it also requires some understanding on the part of the end user.

MEDLINE for End Users

The main problem for end users is language—what words should be used in making a query? Throughout the 1970s and for most of the 1980s, the main users of MEDLINE were the health science librarians who understood its structure. They knew which Medical Subject Headings to use, when to also use the text words that might be in relevant titles and abstracts, and how to draw upon the other indexing elements that are built into MEDLINE. These mediated searches were helpful to the clinicians and researchers who used them, but they lacked the convenience we are accustomed to today. With the proliferation of personal computers and development of user-friendly interfaces during the 1980s, MEDLINE became more widely employed. By the early 1990s, most MEDLINE searches were being done by end users, not by librarians or information specialists. A then-popular MEDLINE search interface, GRATEFUL MED (introduced in 1986), was designed for individuals without search training. However, the majority of health professionals did not have the time or inclination to do effective searches (Humphreys 2002).

The invention of the World Wide Web (begun in December 1990 and widely used by the mid-1990s) (Berners-Lee 1999) changed the landscape for INFORMATION STORAGE AND RETRIEVAL. By the end of the 1990s, most health professionals were accustomed to using the Web. Pages on the Web consist of unstructured text and links. Search engines go through these pages and rank them based on the words they contain, the quality and number of links to and from these pages, and other criteria. Although the pages produced by a MEDLINE search look like most other Web pages, they are different in that they represent aspects of the highly structured documents that comprise the MEDLINE database. These documents are indexed uniformly, hierarchically, and accurately. Deliberate and careful use of Medical Subject Headings and other indexing elements in formulating queries is usually a major contributor to complete and precise MEDLINE searches (Coletti and Bleich 2001). Illumination of these indexing tools is the main point of this book. Library-based classes and the excellent tutorials that are built into PubMed also offer an excellent return on the time required to take advantage of them.

Ease of Use. A variety of approaches have been tried to address the problem of users not knowing what words to use in creating a query, the most influential of which is the National Library of Medicine's UNIFIED MEDICAL LANGUAGE SYSTEM, whose purpose is to facilitate the development of computer systems that behave as if they "understand" the meaning of the language of biomedicine and health. The UNIFIED MEDICAL LANGUAGE SYSTEM is establishing links between the concepts named in more than 100 source vocabularies. Among these are the NLM's own Medical Subject Headings (MeSH), the International Statistical Classification of Diseases (ICD-9-CM_2005, ICD-10), the Diagnostic and Statistical Manual of Mental Disorders (DSM-IV), the Systematized Nomenclature of Medicine—Clinical Terms (SNOWMED CT), standard names for clinical drugs (RxNorm), NCBI Taxonomy, the Human Gene Nomenclature Committee (HUGO), Gene Ontology (GO), DXplain, and Online Mendelian Inheritance in Man (OMIM), to name a few.

When the National Library of Medicine (NLM) began offering free Web-based access to MEDLINE in 1997 (previously connect time charges ranged from $15 to $60 per hour), it launched PubMed. PubMed's default query box uses the UNIFIED MEDICAL LANGUAGE SYSTEM to map user queries (entry words) to the Medical Subject Headings that are likely to be appropriate, in addition to the actual words that make up the query. Entry words are also mapped to journal and author names. The current implementation of PubMed contains an array of additional powerful features that are easy to use, but users need to know how they work and when they might be helpful. In the early years, medical librarians received a three-week training in the use of MEDLINE. It was presumed that the clinicians and researchers who would benefit from MEDLINE searches would rely on an intermediary, someone who could operate the computer—and who also understood the way that MEDLINE is constructed. PubMed is easy to use, and its automation delivers good results, for the most part. But the most effective searches are the result of thoughtful preparation. Using MEDLINE is a bit like driving a powerful racing car that has been modified for street use. It can transport you with astonishing speed to places you don't want to go.

PubMed in Context. PubMed is part of the Entrez retrieval system. Entrez, which is all about discovering relationships, began its existence, in 1992, on CD-ROMs, as a retrieval system for a subset of the MEDLINE database and two molecular biology databases (nucleotide sequences and protein sequences). At this writing (mid-2005), Entrez has been expanded to encompass more than two dozen Web-based databases. In addition to lookups within and among these linked databases, Entrez has the ability to look within a database and discover relationships among "related" sequences or PubMed records. In the case of PubMed, each article is stored with a link that will retrieve a pre-calculated set of citations that are "related" to it, based on the words that appear in the title and abstract and the Medical Subject Headings that were assigned in indexing the citation. Thus, the "related articles" link, a powerful new tool for searching, was created when MEDLINE was broadened in scope and recast as Entrez PubMed. Each of the citations found in a MEDLINE search (preferably a good one) can be studied within the context of articles that are "related" to it.

Entrez databases also link among themselves. PubMed citations contain links to free full text articles in PubMed Central (another Entrez literature database), the MeSH Database (more on this in Chapter 3), Bookshelf (the Entrez database of full text books), the NLM Catalog, and other Entrez resources such as Online Mendelian Inheritance in Man (a comprehensive and constantly updated catalog of inherited diseases) and a variety of molecular biology and chemical databases. In addition, there are links out, beyond Entrez, such as the links from most PubMed citations to full text articles provided by the publisher (which usually require either a subscription or a one-time fee) or to PubMed Central. The robust capacity for linkages among the many rapidly-growing Entrez databases was facilitated by NLM's early adoption of a new technology for creating structured information for the Web, XML.

Standards for Structured Information. HTML (HyperText Mark-up Language), the main language for Web pages, consists primarily of text that has been "marked up" to control how it will look in a Web browser and how the links will work. For example, the phrase "Entrez PubMed" could be emphasized (setting it in italic type) by marking it up like this: Entrez PubMed, which would cause it to appear as *Entrez PubMed* in a Web browser. Or, this phrase, "Entrez PubMed" could be marked up so that it appears as a hyperlink that, if viewed in a Web browser, links to PubMed itself: <a href="http://www.pubmed.gov">Entrez PubMed</a>. HTML is a wonderful vehicle for publishing—a Web page can be read on any kind of computer using any kind of operating system, and portions of its content can be linked to other pages on the Web. But HTML does not provide for any way to mark up content for its meaning: A human can look at a list of words and immediately tell whether it is a list of books, a shopping list, or a mailing list; a computer cannot, unless the words have been marked up for meaning. When we see the word "milk" on a sheet of paper, we can immediately tell whether it is an item on a shopping list or a descriptive word about an article on breast feeding. The word "milk" does not usually pose a semantic challenge for us.

In 1997, the World Wide Web Consortium (www.w3.org), which recommends standards for the Web, introduced an elegant new language, XML (eXtensible Mark-up Language), that allows semantic mark-up. With semantic mark-up, authors' names, words in article titles, subject headings applied by indexers, and other attributes of a document can be tagged for their contextual sense. Then a computer can recognize them for what they are. An understanding of the nuts and bolts of XML is not necessary for most of us,* but

---

* XML consists of three parts: a user-created set of rules that define the meaning of markup (the Document Type Description, or DTD), the document itself (XML is one of the display options in PubMed), and a style sheet for rendering the document as HTML or some other format. In 1999, the NLM announced a DTD for MEDLINE documents, as well as an NLMCommon DTD. The DTD for full text journals in PubMed Central established the archival standard for full text journal content. Because of NLM's stature, its freely available DTDs are setting standards for all structured documents that might eventually link to and from NLM resources.

its existence is having a profound impact on INFORMATION STOR-AGE AND RETRIEVAL. PubMed's links to full text articles, to on-line textbooks, and to other resources are continually being extended. Eventually, there will be extensive links, in multiple directions, between computerized patient records, population health databases, other health-related databases, and relevant knowledge sources.

Searching in PubMed and Other MEDLINE Interfaces. To a novice, searching in MEDLINE looks deceptively easy. The user enters the search terms that seem appropriate, clicks "Go," and a bibliographic list quickly appears, along with options for viewing on-line abstracts and detailed information about how the citations were indexed. In most cases, there are links to full-text electronic versions of articles (sometimes free, sometimes requiring a subscription). But the speed of the retrieval and the plethora of citations proffered can be deceiving. More often than not, the list is disappointing. It is often either too long to read or implausibly short. Many of the references are irrelevant to the purpose of the inquiry, or papers that ought to be there are missing. Successful searching requires knowledge of the vocabulary and grammar that have been carefully developed for querying this huge database. It also requires practice and critical thought.

References

Note: An explanation for the additional information supplied with each journal citation will be provided in Chapter 2.

Barnard GW and Abbott C (1963). *Information Storage and Retrieval: A Survey.* Wright-Patterson Air Force Base, Ohio, Biomedical Laboratory, 6570th Aerospace Medical Research Laboratories, Aeorospace Medical Division, Air Force Systems Command *[Report accessed at the University of California at Berkeley].*

Berners-Lee T (1999). *Weaving the Web: The Original Design and Ultimate Destiny of the World Wide Web by Its Inventor.* New York, HarperCollins.

Billings JS (1879). Prospectus. *Index Medicus.* New York, F. Leypoldt: 1-2.

Chapman CB (1987). John Shaw Billings, 1838-1913: nineteenth century giant. *Bull NY Acad Med* 63(4): 386-409. **MeSH Terms:** HISTORY OF MEDICINE, 19TH CENT.; HISTORY OF MEDICINE, 20TH CENT.; *LIBRARIES, MEDICAL (subheading: history); MEDLARS (subheading: history); NATIONAL LIBRARY OF MEDICINE (U.S.) (subheading: history); NEW YORK CITY; PORTRAITS; UNITED STATES. **Publication Type:** historical article; biography; journal article. PMID: 3304491

Coletti MH and Bleich HL (2001). Medical subject headings used to search the biomedical literature. *J Am Med Inform Assoc.* 2001 Jul-Aug;8(4):317-23. Erratum in: *J Am Med Inform Assoc* 2001 Nov-Dec;8(6):597. **MeSH Terms:** ABSTRACTING AND INDEXING (subheading: history); HISTORY, 19TH CENTURY; HISTORY, 20TH CENTURY; *INFORMATION STORAGE AND RETRIEVAL (subheadings: history; methods); INTERNET; *MEDLARS (subheading: history); *MEDLINE (subheading: history); *SUBJECT HEADINGS; VOCABULARY, CONTROLLED; **Publication Type:** historical article; journal article. PMID: 11418538

Cummings MM (1966). Books, computers and medicine (contributions of a friend of Sir William Osler). *Med Hist* 10(2): 130-7. **MeSH Terms:** *COMPUTERS; HISTORY OF MEDICINE, 19TH CENT.; *NATIONAL LIBRARY OF MEDICINE (U.S.) (subheading: history); *PUNCHED-CARD SYSTEMS (subheading: history); UNITED STATES. **Publication Type:** historical article; biography; journal article. PMID: 5325871

Garrison FH (1915). *John Shaw Billings: A Memoir.* New York, G.P. Putnam's Sons.

Humphreys BL, Lindberg DA, Schoolman HM, Barnett GO (1998). The Unified Medical Language System: an informatics research collaboration. *J Am Med Inform Assoc.* 1998 Jan-Feb;5(1):1-11. **MeSH Terms:** COMPUTER COMMUNICATION NETWORKS; HISTORY, 20TH CENTURY; HOSPITAL INFORMATION SYSTEMS; SYSTEMS INTEGRATION; *UNIFIED MEDICAL LANGUAGE SYSTEM (subheadings: history, organization & administration, trends); **Publication Type:** historical article; journal article. PMID: 9452981

Humphreys BL (2002). Adjusting to progress: interactions between the

National Library of Medicine and health sciences librarians, 1961-2001. *J Med Libr Assoc.* 2002 Jan;90(1):4-20. **MeSH Terms:** HISTORY, 20TH CENTURY; *INFORMATION SERVICES (subheadings: history*, trends); INFORMATION STORAGE AND RETRIEVAL (subheading: history); *LIBRARIANS (subheading: history); *LIBRARIES, MEDICAL (subheadings: history, organization & administration, trends); *NATIONAL LIBRARY OF MEDICINE (U.S.) (subheadings: history, organization & administration, trends); portraits; United States; **Publication Type:** historical article; journal article; lectures. PMID: 11838459

Lipscomb CE (2000). Medical Subject Headings (MeSH). *Bull Med Libr Assoc.* 2000 Jul;88(3):265-6. **MeSH Terms:** HISTORY, 20TH CENTURY; *MEDLARS (subheading: history); MEDLINE; *NATIONAL LIBRARY OF MEDICINE (U.S.) (subheading: history); *SUBJECT HEADINGS; UNIFIED MEDICAL LANGUAGE SYSTEM; UNITED STATES; **Publication Type:** historical article; journal article. PMID: 10928714

Maulitz RC (1997). Billings in cyberspace: toward the electronic Index-Catalogue. *Bull Hist Med.* 1997 Winter;71(4):689-98. **MeSH Terms:** CATALOGS, LIBRARY; *COMPUTER COMMUNICATION NETWORKS; HISTORY, 19TH CENTURY; HISTORY, 20TH CENTURY; HUMANS *MEDLARS (subheading: history); NATIONAL LIBRARY OF MEDICINE (U.S.) (subheading: history); RESEARCH SUPPORT, NON-U.S. GOV'T; UNITED STATES; **Publication Type:** historical article; journal article. PMID: 9431740

Miles WD (1982). *A History of the National Library of Medicine: The Nation's Treasury of Medical Knowledge.* Bethesda, National Institutes of Health.

NLM (2004). IndexCat (http://indexcat.nlm.nih.gov), an on-line version of the *Index-Catalogue of the Library of the Surgeon-General's Office (Index-Catalogue)* became available on the NLM site in 2004. The *Index-Catalogue* was printed from 1880 - 1961 in five series consisting of 61volumes. It cannot be searched with MeSH, but it will be of great value for historians (Maulitz 1997). For more information, see Kozum LM. IndexCat: Index-Catalogue of the Library of the Surgeon-General's Office, 1880-1961. *NLM Technical Bulletin.* 2004 May-Jun;(338):e8.

Rogers FB (1982). The Origins of MEDLARS. In *A Celebration of Medical History* (L. G. Stevenson, Ed.). Baltimore, Johns Hopkins University Press: 77-84.

Sewell W (1964). Medical subject headings in MEDLARS. *Bull Med Libr Assoc.* 1964 Jan;52:164-70. *[PubMed - OLDMEDLINE for Pre1966: Cannot be searched on-line with MeSH.]* PMID: 14119288

Walker CJ, McKibbon KA, Haynes RB, Ramsden MF (1991). Problems encountered by clinical end users of MEDLINE and GRATEFUL MED. *Bull Med Libr Assoc.* 1991 Jan;79(1):67-9. **MeSH Terms:** *GRATEFUL MED; *MEDLINE; NATIONAL LIBRARY OF MEDICINE (U.S.); ONTARIO; PROBLEM SOLVING; RESEARCH SUPPORT, NON-U.S. GOV'T; RESEARCH SUPPORT, U.S. GOV'T, P.H.S.; UNITED STATES; *USER-COMPUTER INTERFACE; **Publication Type:** journal article. PMID: 1998823

Whittock JM and Larkey SF (1955). *Final Report on Subject Headings and on Subject Indexing.* Baltimore, Welsh Medical Library Indexing Project, Johns Hopkins University *[Mimeographed report, accessed at the University of California, San Francisco].*

2
Searching in MEDLINE

THE main difficulty with MEDLINE is its size. It encompasses descriptions of more than 13 million articles in 4,800 journals dating back to 1966. (PubMed, which consists of MEDLINE plus additional citations, is slightly larger.) Citations containing the information you want to find are probably indexed in MEDLINE, but finding them can be difficult. A search strategy that is too broadly focused will produce an extremely long list of citations, most of which will be unrelated to the question at hand. On the other hand, a search strategy that *seems* specific in its focus—but is flawed in its construction—will give the impression that little is known about the topic in question. The key to asking useful questions of this huge and exquisitely organized database is an appreciation of how its contents are indexed, an overview of which is provided in this chapter.

Like all databases, MEDLINE has a separate *field* for each "data element"—consider them as *indexes* and the index terms that go in them. Author names go in the *Author index*, article titles go in the *Title index*, subject headings go in the *Main Heading (MeSH Terms) index*, publication types go in the *Publication Type index,* and so on. The indexes that will be discussed in this chapter are listed in Table 2-1. Index terms can be used in any combination (and from any combination of indexes) to construct the sort of Boolean searches that were described in Chapter 1. For example, you could search for the intersection of two MeSH terms, or the intersection of a journal title and an author's name. Some of these possibilities will be illustrated in this chapter.

TABLE 2-1
Fields or Indexes That Are Frequently Used in MEDLINE Searches
[and Their Official Abbreviations, or Search Field Tags]

Author   [AU]
Author Address (Affiliation)   [AD]
Date of Publication   [DP]
Full Author [FAU]
Journal Title Abbreviation   [TA]
Language   [LA]
Main Headings (Medical Subject Heading Descriptors
        or MeSH terms)   [MH]
Publication Type   [PT]
PubMed Unique Identifier   [PMID]
Subset   [SB]
Text Word   [TW]
Title   [TI]

Searching in MEDLINE can be far more precise than searching on the Web, because MEDLINE is systematically indexed (Coletti and Bleich 2001). The advent of MEDLINE on the World Wide Web has made searching much easier, because of graphic displays and the capacity for linked information. Search screens can be designed to facilitate complex search strategies with a minimum of keyboard entry. The look and feel of interfaces varies considerably. If you are not already using a particular interface and are unsure about where to start, try PubMed (Appendix A), which is fast, free, easy to use, robust in its options, and has an excellent "MeSH Database" link that will help you use the MeSH terms that best describe the concepts you wish to search. If you are accessing MEDLINE through a teaching institution library that has its own interface to MEDLINE, such as Ovid, start with it, but use its "advanced" interface.

Most MEDLINE interfaces present you with a single entry box. These interfaces usually employ algorithms that map your entry terms to the MeSH terms that some of these words *may* be related to. While this software is helpful, it lacks the ability to discriminate among the several MeSH terms that might be related to your typed entry word(s). Also, as discussed later in this chapter, in the sections on Text Words, uncritical use of entry words in MEDLINE can lead to disappointing results. MEDLINE works best when you deliberately employ the controlled vocabulary of MeSH terms and other indexing features that are built into it.

The best example of a simple but effective entry interface is the default query box in PubMed, which automatically maps entry terms to the indexes that are most likely to be appropriate. This is what happens (see PubMed's Help page for a more detailed explanation): The entry terms are first sent to the MeSH Translation Table, which searches for the most likely Medical Subject Heading (the elaborate organization of Medical Subject Headings is described in the next chapter). If a match for a MeSH term is found, a search is directed to the *MeSH term index,* ORing this with a search for the entry terms in the *Text Word index.* If there is no match in the MeSH Translation Table, then the entry terms are sent to a Journals Translation Table (and if a match is found, the search is run in the *Journal index*). If the entry words cannot be found in these two tables, then the Author index is tried for a match. If no match can be found, all the entry terms are ANDed together and searched in the *All Fields index.* This interface is very fast, and it works surprisingly well, especially if you have an idea of what is going on in the background. A "details" link allows you to see how your entry terms were interpreted, and you can modify your search within the oversized query box that you will see when you follow this link.

After conducting a search, it is helpful to examine the indexing of the citations that seem most useful to you. Citations can be displayed in formats that contain links from journal title abbreviations, MeSH terms, and publication types. These links can be followed to learn more, or to modify your search strategy. First, however, we need to look at how articles are indexed in MEDLINE.

Sample Citation

Each search has its own requirements. To begin to explore the range of possibilities for search strategies, an abridged and annotated version of the MEDLINE display (one of the display options in PubMed) for a sample citation is shown below. After seeing how this sample paper is indexed, you will have a basis for appreciating how these various indexes might be used in constructing search strategies. Several of these strategies will be discussed on the pages that follow.

The sample citation is to an article that was published in the *New England Journal of Medicine* at the end of 2004. The authors—Frank B Hu, Walter C Willett, Tricia Li , Meir J Stampfer, Graham A Colditz, and JoAnn E Manson—used data from a large prospective study (the Nurses' Health Study) to resolve the question of whether or not physical activity might protect against the adverse consequences of excess body weight. The paper's author-written abstract, which is part of its indexing in MEDLINE, describes it more completely. The names of the indexes (search fields) [and their search field tags] are shown below in bold face type. The entries for this paper are shown in regular face type, and my comments are shown *in italics*:

PubMed Unique Identifier [PMID]
15616204
Discussed on page 28

Owner
NLM

Volume [VI]
351

Issue [IP]
26

Publication Date [DP]
2004 Dec 23
Discussed on page 31

Title [TI]
Adiposity as compared with physical activity in predicting mortality among women.

Pagination [PG]
2694-703

Abstract [AB]

BACKGROUND: Whether higher levels of physical activity can counteract the elevated risk of death associated with adiposity is controversial. METHODS: We examined the associations of the body-mass index and physical activity with death among 116,564 women who, in 1976, were 30 to 55 years of age and free of known cardiovascular disease and cancer. RESULTS: During 24 years of follow-up, 10,282 deaths occurred—2370 from cardiovascular disease, 5223 from cancer, and 2689 from other causes. Mortality rates increased monotonically with higher body-mass-index values among women who had never smoked (P for trend <0.001). In combined analyses of all participants, adiposity predicted a higher risk of death regardless of the level of physical activity. Higher levels of physical activity appeared to be beneficial at all levels of adiposity but did not eliminate the higher risk of death associated with obesity. As compared with women who were lean (i.e., they had a body-mass index lower than 25) and active (they spent 3.5 or more hours exercising per week), the multivariate relative risks of death were 1.55 (95 percent confidence interval, 1.42 to 1.70) for lean and inactive women, 1.91 (95 percent confidence interval, 1.60 to 2.30) for women who were obese (defined as a body-mass index of 30 or higher) but active, and 2.42 (95 percent confidence interval, 2.14 to 2.73) for inactive, obese women. Even modest weight gain during adulthood, independent of physical activity, was associated with a higher risk of death. We estimate that excess weight (defined as a body-mass index of 25 or higher) and physical inactivity (less than 3.5 hours of exercise per week) together could account for 31 percent of all premature deaths, 59 percent of deaths from cardiovascular disease, and 21 percent of deaths from cancer among nonsmoking women. CONCLUSIONS: Both increased adiposity and reduced physical activity are strong and independent predictors of death.

Affiliation [AD]

Department of Nutrition, Harvard School of Public Health,
Boston, Copyright 2004 Massachusetts Medical Society. USA.
frank.hu@channing.harvard.edu
Discussed on page 31

Author [AU] & Full Author [FAU]

Hu, Frank B
Hu FB
Willett, Walter C
Willett WC
Li, Tricia
Li T
Stampfer, Meir J
Stampfer MJ
Colditz, Graham A
Colditz GA
Manson, JoAnn E
Manson JE
Discussed on page 29

Language [LA]

eng
Discussed on page 31

Grant Number [GR]

CA87969/CA/NCI
HL24074/HL/NHLBI
HL34594/HL/NHLBI
P30 DK46200/DK/NIDDK

Publication Type [PT]

Journal Article
Discussed on page 40

Place of Publication [PL]

United States
This is the journal's place of publication.

Journal Title Abbreviation [TA]

N Engl J Med
Discussed on page 32

NLM Unique Journal ID [JID]
0255562

Subset [SB]
Abridged Index Medicus (AIM)
Index Medicus Journals (IM)
These are journal collection subsets, described on page 40.

Comment In [CIN]
N Engl J Med. 2004 Dec 23;351(26):2751-3. PMID: 15616210
N Engl J Med. 2004 Dec 23;351(26):2753-5. PMID: 15616211
N Engl J Med. 2005 Mar 31;352(13):1381-4;
　　　　　author reply 1381-4. PMID: 15800238
N Engl J Med. 2005 Mar 31;352(13):1381-4;
　　　　　author reply 1381-4. PMID: 15803527
These are comments about this article. The first one (15616210)
mentions this article but is more concerned with bariatric surgery,
which was the topic of another article in this issue. The second one
(15616211)(Jacobs and Pereira 2004) is more specifically about this
article. The third (15800238) (Calle 2005) was a letter from the
principal investigators of another large prospective study, sponsored
by the American Cancer Society. This letter, published several months
after the original article, supplied additional data that confirm the
independent effects of obesity and physical inactivity in predicting
mortality.

Main Headings from NLM's Medical Subject Headings Controlled Vocabulary (MeSH Terms) [MH]

ADIPOSE TISSUE

ADULT

BODY COMPOSITION

*BODY MASS INDEX

CARDIOVASCULAR DISEASES/mortality

COHORT STUDIES

COMPARATIVE STUDY

*EXERCISE

FEMALE

HUMANS

MIDDLE AGED

*MORTALITY

MULTIVARIATE ANALYSIS

NEOPLASMS/mortality

*OBESITY/complications

RESEARCH SUPPORT, NON-U.S. GOV'T

RESEARCH SUPPORT, U.S. GOV'T, P.H.S.

RISK FACTORS

UNITED STATES/epidemiology

WEIGHT GAIN

MeSH terms are discussed on page 34

Entrez Date [EDAT]

2004/12/24 09:00

This is the date that the citation was added to PubMed. In the case of this citation, it was one day after the publication of the article in the New England Journal of Medicine. Its full indexing for MEDLINE was completed very soon thereafter. (The Entrez Date was on a Friday, Christmas was on Saturday, and the indexing for MEDLINE was completed by Tuesday.) Less prominent journals are not indexed for MEDLINE as quickly as this, but the information supplied by the publisher (citation information and the abstract) is available on the Entrez Date.

Text Words [TW]

Text words, most of which come from the title and abstract, are not displayed like the other elements shown here. See discussion (page 36).

Source [SO]

N Engl J Med 2004 Dec 23;351(26):2694-703.

The practical value of these indexes (fields) and their index entries will be illustrated on the pages that follow.

PubMed Unique Identifier [PMID]

When a citation is entered into PubMed, it is assigned a sequential accession number called the *PubMed Unique Identifier,* or PMID. If you know the PMID, you can use it to quickly find the citation that goes with it. For example, the PMID for the Hu et al citation is 15616204. Typing (or copying and pasting) this number into the PubMed query box and hitting "enter" or "return" will take you to the citation and its abstract. Several PMIDs can be entered at once; no punctuation or qualification is necessary. Anything more than the number(s) may confuse the system.

PMIDs can be a handy way of your annotating your notes, serving as a kind of low-tech ProCite® or EndNote®. I recently received an e-mail that cited a PMID instead of a more standard citation format, or a link to the citation in PubMed. You can even Google a PubMed citation by entering its PMID, though this might lead you to a protein sequence or somewhere else if you click the "I'm Feeling Lucky" button. But PubMed will always take you directly from the PMID to the citation.

Author [AU] & Full Author [FAU]

Authors are indexed by last name and initials. For more recent articles, authors' first names are indexed as well. A search on only the last name of an author will retrieve a list of citations by all authors with that last name. PubMed's automatic term mapping is quite good at recognizing author names: in the case of the lead author to the above citation, it did not matter whether "hu fb" or "hu fb" [au] was entered into the PubMed search box. Both approaches attracted the same 174 citations. Omitting the bracketed search field tags will sometimes retrieve citations that have not yet been indexed for MEDLINE ("PubMed - in process; data supplied by the publisher")—this is helpful when trying to find an article that has been cited in a news report.

More authors are needed to produce a shorter list—hu fb [au] AND willett wc [au] AND li t [au] found three citations, one of which was the above-described citation (Hu et al 2004).

Starting with 2002, first author names are indexed as well, if the full name is available in the article. These can be entered in natural or inverted order: Frank B Hu or Hu Frank B. The search field tag for full author is [fau].

If you know the name of someone who has published in the area you are seeking to know more about, then you may want to see a list of that author's publications, listed in reverse chronological order. This can be quite useful if the author is a major contributor to the field you are researching. Also, there may be instances when you remember a paper only by its author AND the journal in which it was published (for example, Hu et al's *New England Journal of Medicine* paper). This limited bibliographic information is all that you need to find the citation in MEDLINE. Here is how the above paper was located with such limited information:

❖ Searching in the *Author index* under "hu fb" found 174 citations.

❖ When these were limited to citations indexed under "N Engl J Med" in the *Journal Title Abbreviation index*, 7 citations were found, one of which was the "Adiposity as Compared with Physical Activity in Predicting Mortality among Women" paper. In other words, the strategy was hu fb AND n engl j med.

Such author/journal information is typical of the information printed in newspaper and magazine articles that report on "important" medical publications. Newspaper mention of a paper will appear before it is indexed in MEDLINE, but publisher-supplied information may be available in PubMed (search with unqualified terms in the query box). In addition, the news clipping can be saved in your reprint files and used later to locate the newsworthy study.

PubMed's "Single Citation Matcher" is a convenient fill-in-the-blank form that allows you to input any information you might have on hand, such as journal title, article title words, author, date, or volume. It can be reached from a link on the main search screen.

Affiliation [AD]

Information from the lead author's affiliation is included in the abstract, citation, and other displays in PubMed. Affiliation information often includes the institution name, an e-mail address, and a street address with zip code. Any of these can be searched in PubMed and other versions of MEDLINE. For example, the search strategy "ucsf [ad]" (without the quotes) finds citations that include e-mail addresses at ucsf.edu in the affiliation field. Similarly, many researchers from the San Francisco Department of Public Health are located at zip code 94102, and the search strategy "94102 [ad]" (without the quotes) finds publications describing their work. To find research from the Cleveland Clinic, these two words need to be ANDed together (cleveland [ad] AND clinic [ad]).

Language [LA]

The majority of the papers indexed in MEDLINE were written in English. Although foreign language papers should not be discounted, limiting a search to English language papers is a useful device for narrowing a search. French, German, Italian, Spanish, Japanese, and Russian are a few of the more than 40 non-English languages that are indexed in MEDLINE, and searches can be limited to any single language or combination of languages. Non-English language papers frequently include abstracts that are written in English.

Publication Date [DP]

The *Publication Date* is listed as a four-digit year, abbreviated month, and then day—for the above-described article by Hu et al, it was "2004 Dec 23." In most searches, you will be looking for a particular year or range of years.

Because MEDLINE is so large, some interfaces divide it up into a current file (usually the last three to five years), which is the default (what you see first), with older files such as 1995–2000, 1990–1994, 1985–1989, 1980–1984, 1975–1979, and 1966–1974 as additional search options. PubMed, by default, searches the entire MEDLINE database, plus additional citations that are not yet fully indexed (data supplied by publisher) or never will be indexed because they are beyond MEDLINE's scope, as well as older, pre-1966 citations. PubMed allows you to limit searches within a range of publication dates, or by Entrez date—the date the publication was added to PubMed. PubMed's results are listed in reverse chronological order (except, of course, the results displayed from the "related articles" link).

You will probably be interested in the latest information, but older publications are frequently invaluable. For example, a 1993 paper by McGinnis and Foege, published in *JAMA: Journal of the American Medical Association,* re-framed the leading causes of death in the United States (heart disease, cancer, stroke, accidents, chronic obstructive pulmonary disease, pneumonia, diabetes, suicide, cirrhosis, and AIDS) in terms of their underlying risk factors or population-based determining causes (tobacco, diet/inactivity, alcohol, infectious agents, environmental toxins, guns, unsafe sex, motor vehicles, and illicit drugs). These underlying preventable causes accounted for half of all the mortality in the United States (McGinnis and Foege 1993). Although others have provided a more recent update to this analysis (Mokdad 2004), McGinnis and Foege's seminal paper (cited in more than a thousand journal articles and in many books) is old enough to be overlooked by a search strategy that focused only on the most recent literature. Some papers are significant enough that they are subsequently republished—for example, Goeffrey Rose's "Sick Individuals and Sick Populations" (Rose 1985; Rose 2001a; Rose 2001b). Subsequent republications are indexed separately as new publications.

Journal Title Abbreviation [TA]

The *Journal Title Abbreviation index* entry for Hu et al's paper is "N Engl J Med." If you are looking for a particular paper and know the journal that it was published in—and its Journal Title Abbreviation— you can use this index in combination with one or more MeSH terms, or an author's name or affilliation to quickly find the citation.

You will see journal title abbreviations in your search results. Some of these may be unfamiliar to you. A mouse-over will display the full name when you are in PubMed's Summary, Abstract, or Citation displays. In the Abstract and Citation displays, the journal title abbreviations appear as links. These links can be followed to find more information in the Journals Database, or to create a new search strategy.

Many interfaces to MEDLINE contain software that will map a search entry from its full name to its standard abbreviation; accordingly, the *New England Journal of Medicine* automatically becomes N Engl J Med. To save yourself keystrokes and to avoid problems, it is best to use these standard abbreviations. PubMed's "Journals Database" can help you with journal names and their abbreviations. Journal title abbreviations for important clinical journals are listed in Appendix B.

Limiting searches to a particular journal or list of journals is also useful in making optimal use of the journals within your own personal library. Some MEDLINE interfaces allow you to set up a personalized journal list.

Recall Versus Precision

The index terms discussed thus far are helpful if you know something about the citation you wish to find. The more common situation, however, is one in which you are looking for information that might answer a particular question. Search strategies can be formulated in different ways depending on whether you wish to be more precise or more comprehensive. The constant dilemma in searching is knowing whether a narrower or a broader search strategy would be better. Informatics researchers have given a lot of thought to this dilemma. Recall and precision are the concepts that informatics researchers use in describing the percentage of relevant articles retrieved:

The *recall ratio* is the number of relevant references retrieved divided by all of the relevant references in MEDLINE.

The *precision ratio* is the number of relevant references retrieved divided by the number of references retrieved.

Ideally, we want a high recall ratio (we don't want to miss any relevant references), and we also want a high precision ratio (we don't want to see a lot of junk in our retrieval results). Unfortunately, recall and precision are inversely related. A broadly focused strategy will improve recall at the expense of precision. A precisely focused strategy may miss things. You will need to employ a variety of strategies to optimize the balance between recall and precision, and the strategies you chose will depend on your search goals. Sometimes you will want to find everything about a topic. Sometimes you will want just a few relevant papers. The key to effective searching is understanding MeSH terms, Text Words, Publication Types, and the other indexing features that are built into MEDLINE.

Main Headings [MH] from NLM's Medical Subject Headings Controlled Vocabulary (MeSH Terms)

The 20 MeSH terms (out of more than 23,000) that most specifically describe Hu et al's "Adiposity as Compared with Physical Activity in Predicting Mortality among Women" paper are shown on pages 27-28. The paper was read by a skilled subject analyst at the National Library of Medicine, who, following the Library's carefully defined rules for their use, assigned them. For this paper, BODY MASS INDEX, EXERCISE, and MORTALITY appear with asterisks in front of them, indicating that these are the major topics under which the paper is indexed. This is primarily a paper about the intersections of these concepts. These are the subjects under which the paper would have been indexed in the *Index Medicus,* the printed version of MEDLINE, if it were still in print.

To discover papers like Hu et al's "Adiposity as Compared with Physical Activity in Predicting Mortality among Women" paper, you would have to anticipate their existence, and you would have to imagine what MeSH terms might characterize such papers. You would have to be wondering if there were any studies that compared physical activity (the authors' term, which is captured by EXERCISE) with adiposity (the authors' term, which is captured by OBESITY—or, more precisely, BODY MASS INDEX) in predicting MORTALITY. Here is a strategy that makes use of some of these MeSH terms*:

❖ Searching in the *MeSH index* for EXERCISE found 30,476 citations.

❖ Searching for "exercise" [MeSH] AND "obesity" [MeSH] found 2,726 citations.

❖ Searching for "exercise" [MeSH] AND "obesity" [MeSH] AND "mortality" [MeSH] found 27 citations, one of which was Hu et al's and another of which was an invited editorial that accompanied it in the same issue (Jacobs and Pereira 2004).

In addition to the dozen or so MeSH terms that describe the concepts embodied in each paper, the indexers often assign *subheadings* or *qualifiers* to them, allowing the user to narrow a search to a specific aspect of a Medical Subject Heading. For example, OBESITY doesn't describe this paper as well as does OBESITY with the subheading "complications" applied to it. Subheadings will be discussed in the next chapter.

This controlled vocabulary of MeSH terms and their associated subheadings requires some practice, but the link to the "MeSH Database" in PubMed will take you to an easy-to-use interface for

---

*The official search field tag [MH] is interchangeable with [MeSH], and neither is case sensitive)—[mh] or [mesh] work as well as [MH] or [MeSH] or [MeSH Terms].

building MeSH-based search strategies. You can also display your results in a format that will show the MeSH terms assigned to an article. Links from each of these can be followed to find information in the MeSH Database, or they can serve as the basis for a new search. You will quickly learn the MeSH terms that pertain to your particular areas of interest. Because MeSH terms are so important to MEDLINE, they are discussed in greater detail in an entire chapter, which follows. To illustrate the descriptive richness of MeSH terms, they have been added to the more traditional bibliographic information shown for each of the references cited in this book. These expanded references are listed at the end of each chapter.

Text Words [TW]

The *Text Word* (key word) index entries for Hu et al's "Adiposity as Compared with Physical Activity in Predicting Mortality among Women" paper are not systematically displayed on pages 24–28 with the other indexing elements for this paper. However, they can be imagined as an alphabetic list of the words that appear in the title and the abstract, in addition to the MeSH terms and subheadings that were assigned to the paper, along with other indexing terms. Duplicate words are eliminated, and any of more than 300 "stopwords" such as "the," "and," "was," or "for" are also eliminated.

The *Text Word index* appears easier to use than the *MeSH terms index*, because it allows you to simply guess which words might be most useful for searching, but it is more likely to point you in the wrong direction or cause you to miss useful citations. MeSH terms, on the other hand, are more likely to lead you to the citations you want, but they require some knowledge of this specific vocabulary. Here are some search strategies that make use of text words from Hu et al's paper (compare with the search on page 35):

❖ Searching for "physical activity" found 74,641 citations.

❖ The authors' term "adiposity" isn't likely to come to mind, but we might use "obesity" instead. Both "adiposity" and "obesity" appear as words in the abstract. PubMed maps "obesity" to "obesity" [MeSH] OR "obesity" [Text Word]. Searching for "physical activity" AND "obesity" finds 3,429 citations.

❖ Searching for "physical activity" AND "obesity" AND "mortality" as unqualified text words found 301 citations (roughly ten times as many as found in the MeSH-based search on page 35), one of which was Hu et al's. Among the many papers not captured by the search on page 35 were some that had not yet been indexed for MEDLINE, as well as a large number of papers that were not concerned with comparing the relative importance of "physical activity" and "obesity" on "mortality." Unqualified entry terms are mapped as [MeSH Terms] OR [Text Words], which greatly increases recall (see pages 33-34).

Text Words and the Recall/Precision Dilemma

The expanded recall in the above search strategy was accompanied by a lack of precision. For example, one of the citations that was captured was a report from the CDC, published in *MMWR. Morbidity and Mortality Weekly Report,* entitled "Perceptions of neighborhood characteristics and leisure-time physical inactivity—Austin/Travis County, Texas, 2004" (CDC 2004). Although "physical activity" AND "obesity" AND "mortality" all appeared as words in the abstract, these were not the main concepts examined in the paper. Hence, it was not found in the MeSH-based search on page 35.

The words that authors use in creating a title and abstract for their paper are useful, and they might be essential in augmenting the characterization of a paper by its formal indexing with MeSH terms. For example, acronyms (if you already know them) will help you to locate papers whose authors employ them. Similarly, a new concept will not be specifically described by a MeSH term (though papers about such concepts will be indexed under a broader heading that encompasses the concept). If you know or suspect such concept and can name it, use Text Words (unqualified entry terms) in your search. Because the plural form or another word variant might be used as a Text Word, you might consider using the truncation symbol (* for PubMed, $ for Ovid); truncation turns off automatic term mapping in PubMed.

Remember, however, that Text Words are not weighted for their significance to the paper. Also, various authors might use the same words to mean different things. One author might use the word "interactions" to describe the way that clinicians and patients relate to one another (a concept captured by the MeSH term PHYSICIAN-PATIENT RELATIONS), while another might use it in describing drug interactions (a concept captured by DRUG INTERACTIONS). On the other hand, various authors use different words to describe the same thing. For example, some authors use the word "tobacco" in reference to the large literature on the health effects of "tobacco smoking" and "cigarettes." This literature is systematically indexed under SMOKING (and there are other concepts, such as TOBACCO SMOKE POLLUTION or TOBACCO USE DISORDER or SMOKING CESSA-TION, that might be pertinent to a search). If "tobacco" were used in a Text Word search, the results would include papers indexed under the MeSH term TOBACCO in addition to papers containing "tobacco" in the title or abstract. This would lead to disappointing results, because TOBACCO is used for indexing papers concerning the tobacco plant.

Even when there is no ambiguity, it is best to find the MeSH term that captures the concept you are searching. Though "nose bleed," "nose bleeds," and "nosebleed" all map automatically to EPISTAXIS, "nosebleeds" does not. A search that relied on "nose-bleeds" would miss most of the citations concerning this topic.

When "nosebleeds" is used as an entry term in the MeSH database, nothing is found, but "nosebleed" and other variants are suggested. These lead to EPISTAXIS.

Text Words are not as good at capturing concepts as MeSH terms, but they can add precision when searching for specific words or acronyms that you know are being used to describe an area of inquiry. For example, a search for "ALLHAT" leads to more than 200 citations concerning the "Antihypertensive and Lipid-Lowering Treatment to Prevent Heart Attack" trial. On the other hand, acronyms or phrases can produce incomplete results. For example, "Nurses' Health Study" leads to dozens of papers from this important study, but the paper by Hu et al is not among them, because the authors did not use these words in the title or abstract. (They describe the Nurses' Health Study within the Methods section of their paper.) A search for the Hu et al citation that used "Nurses' Health Study" as Text Words would gain precision at the expense of recall; their paper cannot be found with this strategy.

Related Articles in PubMed

Whatever strategy you might use, you will see some citations that appear more useful than others. To see more articles like the ones that seem most useful, PubMed offers a "related articles" link. Following this link creates a new search, based on a powerful algorithm that employs all the MeSH terms and text words from the starting article. The articles near the top of the results are usually excellent matches. This is an extremely useful tool. The most useful of these "related articles" can be displayed in the citation format or other display format that will show you the MeSH terms that were used in their indexing. These MeSH terms can be used in subsequent searches. Using them to construct your search strategy within PubMed's MeSH Database (linked from the left-hand side of the main screen) will allow you to learn more about these MeSH terms, such as their precise meaning and place within the hierarchy of other terms (described in the next chapter).

Publication Type [PT]

Each citation in MEDLINE is categorized by the indexers at the National Library of Medicine as belonging to one or more *Publication Type,* such as "journal article," "editorial," "letter," "controlled clinical trial," "meta-analysis," "practice guideline," or "review," to name a few. Publication Types are an extremely useful way to limit searches. For example, if you wanted to advise a patient about SMOKING CESSATION, you could limit the more than 7,000 articles in MEDLINE that are indexed under this MeSH term to the roughly 50 that are also indexed as being a "practice guideline." Searches can be limited by *Publication Type* by using the "Limits" option in PubMed. *Publication Types* are discussed in more detail in Chapter 4.

Journal Collections

Instead of searching for articles within all of the more than 4,600 journals indexed in MEDLINE, you can limit your search to one of several journal groupings: Nursing Journals, Dental Journals, PubMed Central (free full text), or Core Clinical Journals (the Abridged Index Medicus). These are available from the Limits tab in PubMed, using the Subsets option. Journal collection limits can also be set from PubMed's Special Queries page.

The Abridged Index Medicus (AIM) consists of more than a hundred clinical journals that the National Library of Medicine considers to be the core clinical journals for a medical library. These are listed in Appendix B. The Abridged Index Medicus is really a historical artifact, dating back to the origins of MEDLINE; it was a way of allocating once-scarce computer resources. The Abridged Index Medicus subset is sometimes a useful way to limit unwieldy search results with a crude first cut that probably will not eliminate the "most important" journals, but be careful—many important journals are excluded from the Abridged Index Medicus. If you are using a MEDLINE interface that allows you to set up a personalized journal list (essentially your own subset), you might review the Abridged Index Medicus subset in Appendix B as a start.

PubMed's Subject Subset [SB] Limits

PubMed allows you to select any of several pre-constructed strategies to limit your search by topic area. Currently available subject
subsets are AIDS, bioethics, cancer, complementary medicine, history of medicine, space life sciences, and toxicology. Use PubMed's
Limits option or Special Queries page to access them.

PubMed's Clinical Queries Page

Carefully evaluated combinations of MeSH terms, Publication
Types, and text words are the basis for PubMed's Clinical Queries
filters. These can be reached from a link on the main search screen.
Several types of filters are currently available. One of them filters
your entry terms to find categories of clinical studies. You select
the category (therapy, diagnosis, etiology, or prognosis) and specify
the emphasis (broad or narrow). Another filter retrieves citations
for systematic reviews, meta-analyses, reviews of clinical trials,
evidence-based medicine, consensus development conferences, and
guidelines. Still another can help you with medical genetics searches.
The methodology for these filters is explained in PubMed Help.
There will be more of these filters in the future.

As with any search, the quality of your results will be influenced
by the entry terms that you use.

PubMed's Special Queries Page

PubMed's Special Queries page, which can be reached from a link
on the main search screen, is a directory of topic-specific queries.
These queries employ a variety of strategies and resources. Some
of the strategies you will find here—Journal Groupings, Subject
Subsets, and Clinical Queries—are described above. Others, many
of which employ special search filters, include Health Services
Research, Cancer Topic Searches, Complementary and Alterna-
tive Medicine, Healthy People 2010, ALTBIB (Bibliography on
Alternatives to Animal Testing), History of Medicine in PubMed,

MedlinePlus Health Topics (aimed at consumers), and TOXNET (more than a dozen toxicological databases).

References

Calle EE, Teras LR, Thun MJ (2005). Adiposity and physical activity as predictors of mortality. *N Engl J Med.* 2005 Mar 31;352(13):1381-4; author reply 1381-4. **MeSH Terms:** ADIPOSE TISSUE; COHORT STUDIES; *EXERCISE; FEMALE; HUMANS; MALE; *MORTALITY; *OBESITY (subheading: complications); **Publication Type:** comment; letter. PMID: 15800238

Centers for Disease Control and Prevention (CDC) (2004). Perceptions of neighborhood characteristics and leisure-time physical inactivity--Austin/Travis County, Texas, 2004. MMWR Morb Mortal Wkly Rep. 2005 Sep 23;54(37):926-8. **MeSH Terms:** ADULT; BEHAVIORAL RISK FACTOR SURVEILLANCE SYSTEM; FEMALE; HUMANS; *LEISURE ACTIVITIES; MALE; MIDDLE AGED; *PHYSICAL FITNESS; *RESIDENCE CHARACTERISTICS; TEXAS. **Publication Type:** journal article. PMID: 16177684

Coletti MH and Bleich HL (2001). Medical subject headings used to search the biomedical literature. *J Am Med Inform Assoc.* 2001 Jul-Aug;8(4):317-23. **MeSH Terms:** ABSTRACTING AND INDEXING (subheading: history); HISTORY, 19TH CENTURY; HISTORY, 20TH CENTURY; *INFORMATION STORAGE AND RETRIEVAL (subheadings: history; methods); INTERNET; *MEDLARS (subheading: history); *MEDLINE (subheading: history); *SUBJECT HEADINGS; VOCABULARY, CONTROLLED; **Publication Type:** historical article; journal article. PMID: 11418538

Hu FB, Willett WC, Li T, Stampfer MJ, Colditz GA, Manson JE (2004). Adiposity as compared with physical activity in predicting mortality among women. *N Engl J Med.* 2004 Dec 23;351(26):2694-703. **MeSH Terms:** ADIPOSE TISSUE; ADULT; BODY COMPOSITION; *BODY MASS INDEX; CARDIOVASCULAR DISEASES (subheading: mortality); COHORT STUDIES; COMPARATIVE STUDY; *EXERCISE; FEMALE; HUMANS; MIDDLE AGED; *MORTALITY; MULTIVARIATE ANALYSIS; NEOPLASMS (subheading: mortality); *OBESITY (subheading: complications); RESEARCH SUPPORT, NON-U.S. GOV'T; RESEARCH SUPPORT, U.S. GOV'T,

P.H.S.; RISK FACTORS; UNITED STATES (subheading: epidemiology); WEIGHT GAIN; **Publication Type:** journal article. PMID: 15616204

Jacobs DR Jr, Pereira MA (2004). Physical activity, relative body weight, and risk of death among women. *N Engl J Med.* 2004 Dec 23;351(26):2753-5. **MeSH Terms:** ADIPOSE TISSUE (subheading: physiology); *BODY MASS INDEX; *BODY WEIGHT (subheading: physiology); CHRONIC DISEASE; CONFOUNDING FACTORS (EPIDEMIOLOGY); *EXERCISE (subheading: physiology); FEMALE; HUMANS; MALE; *MORTALITY; *OBESITY (subheading: complications); PHYSICAL FITNESS; RISK FACTORS; WEIGHT LOSS; **Publication Type:** comment; editorial. PMID: 15616211

McGinnis JM and Foege WH (1993). Actual causes of death in the United States. *JAMA.* 1993 Nov 10;270(18):2207-12. **MeSH Terms:** ACCIDENTS, TRAFFIC (subheading: mortality); ALCOHOL DRINKING (subheading: mortality); *CAUSE OF DEATH; COMMUNICABLE DISEASES (subheading: mortality); DATA COLLECTION; DIET (subheading: mortality); ENVIRONMENTAL POLLUTANTS; FIREARMS (subheading: statistics & numerical data); HUMAN; *MORTALITY; PHYSICAL FITNESS; SEX BEHAVIOR (subheading: statistics & numerical data); SMOKING (subheading: mortality); SUBSTANCE-RELATED DISORDERS (subheading: mortality); UNITED STATES (subheading: epidemiology); **Publication Type:** journal article. PMID: 8411605

Mokdad AH, Marks JS, Stroup DF, Gerberding JL (2004). Actual causes of death in the United States, 2000. *JAMA.* 2004 Mar 10;291(10):1238-45. **MeSH Terms:** ACCIDENTS, TRAFFIC (subheading: mortality); ALCOHOL DRINKING; *CAUSE OF DEATH (subheading: trends); COMMUNICABLE DISEASES (subheading: mortality); DIET; HUMANS; PHYSICAL FITNESS; POISONING (subheading: mortality); RISK FACTORS; SEXUAL BEHAVIOR; SMOKING (subheading: mortality); SUBSTANCE-RELATED DISORDERS; UNITED STATES (subheading: epidemiology); WOUNDS, GUNSHOT (subheading: mortality); **Publication Type:** journal article, review, review, multicase. PMID: 15010446

Rose G (1985). Sick individuals and sick populations. *Int J Epidemiol.* 1985 Mar;14(1):32-8. **MeSH Terms:** *CARDIOVASCULAR DISEASES (subheadings: epidemiology; prevention & control); CROSS-SECTIONAL STUDIES; *EPIDEMIOLOGIC METHODS; HUMANS; POPULATION SURVEILLANCE; RISK; **Publication Type:** journal article. PMID: 3872850

Rose G (2001a). Sick individuals and sick populations. *Int J Epidemiol.* 2001 Jun;30(3):427-32; discussion 433-4. **MeSH Terms:** CARDIOVAS-CULAR DISEASES (subheadings: epidemiology; etiology; prevention & control); *CAUSALITY; DISEASE SUSCEPTIBILITY; *EPIDEMIOLOGIC METHODS; HUMANS; INCIDENCE; POPULATION SURVEILLANCE; RISK; **Publication Type:** journal article. PMID: 11416056

Rose G (2001b). Sick individuals and sick populations. 1985. *Bull World Health Organ.* 2001;79(10):990-6. **MeSH Terms:** *CARDIOVASCU-LAR DISEASES (subheadings: epidemiology; prevention & control); CAUSALITY, *EPIDEMIOLOGIC STUDIES, GREAT BRITAIN (subheading: epidemiology); HISTORY, 20TH CENTURY; HUMANS; INCIDENCE; POPULATION SURVEILLANCE, PREVENTIVE MEDICINE (subheading: history);*PUBLIC HEALTH PRACTICE (subheading: history); **Publication Type:** biography, classical article, historical article, journal article. PMID: 11693983

3

Medical Subject Headings (MeSH)

When a physician has observed (or thinks he has observed) a fact, or has evolved from his inner consciousness a theory which he wishes to examine by the light of the medical literature, he is often very much at a loss to know how to begin, even if he has a large library accessible for the purpose.

The information he desires may be in the volume next to his hand, but how is he to know that? And even when the usual subject-catalogue is placed before him he finds it very difficult to use it, especially when, as is often the case, he has by no means a well defined idea as to what it is he wishes to look for. Upon the title page of the Washington City Directory is printed the following aphorism, "To find a name you must know how to spell it." This has a very extensive application in medical bibliography. To find accounts similar to your own rare case you must know what your own case is.

John Shaw Billings (1881)

DURING the late 1990s, a worker at the San Francisco Department of Public Health received an e-mail asking whether there were any data linking the use of cell phones to accidents caused by distracted drivers. The City's Board of Supervisors was considering a regulation to ban the use of car and cell phones while driving. Using a Web-based source of MeSH information, "car phones" was typed in, but none of the MeSH terms that came up were appropriate. Similarly, neither "cell phones" nor "phones" seemed related to a useful MeSH term. But typing in "telephones" showed that TELEPHONE is a MeSH term. [*Note:* At the time, CELLULAR PHONE (introduced in 2003) was not yet a

MeSH term. The implications of this MeSH vocabulary change are discussed on page 53.] Then, typing "accidents" showed that AC-CIDENTS is a MeSH term, and at the same time, it became apparent that ACCIDENTS, TRAFFIC is also a MeSH term—one that would be more appropriate to the query. Searching for ACCIDENTS, TRAFFIC AND TELEPHONE produced a list of 27 citations, many of them with abstracts. A cursory review of these abstracts suggested that the use of cell phones may indeed be a risk for traffic accidents (Redelmeier and Tibshirani 1997; Violanti 1998), though cell phones are useful for quickly reporting traffic accidents and dangerous situations (Chapman and Schofield 1998). One of these articles (Redelmeier and Tibshirani 1997) was in a copy of the *New England Journal of Medicine* that was already in the searcher's office, and in the same issue was a carefully reasoned editorial (Maclure and Mittleman 1997), another of the 27 citations found by this search. Within a fairly short amount of time, the worker was able to respond to the e-mail, sending information and reliable sources to inform the debate. The most important part of this search was determining that it would be about ACCIDENTS, TRAFFIC AND TELEPHONE.

Medical Subject Headings (MeSH) Vocabulary

ACCIDENTS, TRAFFIC and TELEPHONE are among the Main Headings described in Table 3-1. ACCIDENTS, TRAFFIC belongs to the Biological Sciences Category (G), and TELEPHONE belongs to the Information Science Category (L). Here is a brief overview of the MeSH vocabulary that is outlined in Table 3-1:

Main Headings (MeSH Terms) and Subheadings. Main Headings (MeSH terms) are the National Library of Medicine's controlled vocabulary for describing biomedical knowledge. The terms described in the above example are variously called "Main Headings" or "MeSH Headings" or "Descriptors" or "MeSH terms." An average of 10 to 12 of them are applied to each article that is indexed in MEDLINE. They represent concepts that are reliably named using this controlled vocabulary, and there are more than 23,000 of these

TABLE 3–1
MeSH Categories (2006)

The Main Headings, of which there were nearly 24,000 in 2006, are hierarchically arranged (in branching form, hence the term "trees") to show how they are related to one another, and these Main Headings are often qualified with subheadings when they are applied to articles by the indexers.

Main Headings (Descriptors, MeSH Terms) [MH]

    A. Anatomy Category

    B. Organisms Category

    C. Diseases Category

    D. Chemicals and Drugs Category

    E. Analytical, Diagnostic and Therapeutic Techniques and Equipment Category

    F. Psychiatry and Psychology Category

    G. Biological Sciences Category

    H. Physical Sciences Category

    I. Anthropology, Education, Sociology and Social Phenomena Category

    J. Technology and Food and Beverages Category

    K. Humanities Category

    L. Information Science Category

    M. Persons Category

    N. Health Care Category

    V. Publication Type Category

    Z. Geographical Locations Category

Other MeSH Categories

    Subheadings

    Supplementary Concept Records

    Pharmacological Action [PA]

    Publication Type [PT] (within Publication Type Category)

MeSH terms. When the indexers apply these "Main Headings" or "MeSH Headings" or "Descriptors" or "MeSH terms" to an article, they often qualify their use with "subheadings." Subheadings, which represent a distinct category of MeSH, are described on pages 54-58.

Supplementary Concept Records. In addition to the more than 23,000 Main Headings (Descriptors, MeSH terms), there are more than 150,000 supplementary concepts that describe the chemicals and drugs (substance names) and the proteins that are not Main Headings. Supplementary Concepts are discussed on page 61.

Publication Type [PT]. This category of MeSH is a small vocabulary that describes articles by their type of publication (journal article, letter, meta-analysis, review, etc.) rather than the concepts that are contained within them. Publication Types are discussed in the next chapter.

The Main Headings (Descriptors, MeSH terms) depict biomedical concepts that are often intimately related to one another. Therefore, the organization of Main Headings is important.

Organization of Main Headings (MeSH Terms): MeSH Trees

MeSH terms are organized by categories, and these categories are grouped into sub-categories, each of which has further sub-categories, and so on. This organization means that each MeSH term exists in a hierarchical relationship to others. These hierarchies are based on general and ever more specific concepts. Because of the branching of these hierarchies, they are sometimes referred to as "trees." This is clearly illustrated by an example from the Anatomy Category—the relationship of the THUMB to the FINGERS and the HAND, and to other body parts:

All Categories of Medical Subject Headings

A. Anatomy Category
    BODY REGIONS
        EXTREMITIES
           UPPER EXTREMITY
             ARM
             AXILLA
             ELBOW
             FOREARM
             HAND
                FINGERS
                  THUMB
             WRIST
            SHOULDER

Articles whose authors describe various conditions pertaining to the "finger-tip" or "finger-tips" or "finger tips" or "fingertips," etc. are all reliably indexed under FINGERS.

In the above search for information about whether the use of car phones might be linked with accidents, both "ACCIDENTS" and "ACCIDENTS, TRAFFIC" were identified as MeSH terms. "ACCIDENTS, TRAFFIC" was used in the search, because it was more specific to the query than "ACCIDENTS." There are many kinds of ACCIDENTS, one of which is ACCIDENTS, TRAFFIC:

All Categories of Medical Subject Headings
  G. Biological Sciences Category
      ENVIRONMENT AND PUBLIC HEALTH
        PUBLIC HEALTH
          ACCIDENTS
            ACCIDENT PREVENTION
              SAFETY
                SAFETY MANAGEMENT
            ACCIDENTAL FALLS
            ACCIDENTS, AVIATION
            ACCIDENTS, HOME

ACCIDENTS, OCCUPATIONAL
ACCIDENTS, RADIATION
ACCIDENTS, RADIATION
ACCIDENTS, TRAFFIC
DROWNING
NEAR DROWNING

Similarly, the clinical condition ANGINA PECTORIS exists in relation to broader, narrower and other MeSH terms, all of which exist in hierarchical relationship to one another:

MYOCARDIAL ISCHEMIA
CORONARY DISEASE
ANGINA PECTORIS
ANGINA PECTORIS, VARIANT
ANGINA, UNSTABLE
MICROVASCULAR ANGINA
CORONARY ANEURYSM
CORONARY ARTERIOSCLEROSIS
CORONARY STENOSIS
CORONARY THROMBOSIS
CORONARY VASOSPASM
ANGINA PECTORIS, VARIANT
MYOCARDIAL INFARCTION
MYOCARDIAL STUNNING
SHOCK, CARDIOGENIC

In addition, because of all the branching that occurs at various levels of these MeSH term hierarchies, the same term can appear on more than one branch. For example, ANGINA PECTORIS appears under MYOCARDIAL ISCHEMIA, as depicted above, and it also appears in two other places: Because MYOCARDIAL ISCHEMIA appears on two separate branches (as a branch of HEART DISEASES and as a branch of ISCHEMIA), ANGINA PECTORIS is a branch of each of these. In addition, one of the branches of PAIN is CHEST

PAIN, and ANGINA PECTORIS is a branch there as well. In all three cases, ANGINA PECTORIS means the same thing. It exists in three places, because the concepts that MeSH terms represent exist in various relationships to one another. This multiple placement of a MeSH term is akin to your name being the same but appearing in different places, depending on whether you are being classified as an employee, a student, an owner of a motor vehicle, a spouse, etc. In NLM's MeSH Browser, descriptors are numbered to depict where in the tree they are. ANGINA PECTORIS is C14.280.647.250.125, C14.907.553.470.250.125, AND C23.888.646.215.500. These numbers have no inherent significance—they change when new concepts are added or when the hierarchical arrangement is shifted to accommodate new MeSH terms. It really does look like branches on a tree, except that each branch of the tree is numbered. The important thing is that each concept is named consistently, and this makes for consistent retrieval of information.

Broader/Narrower MeSH & Explosions

Indexers are instructed to assign the MeSH terms that most specifically describe the paper they are indexing. From a user's standpoint, this generally leads to the most precise search results. However, there are circumstances when you may wish to use a broader MeSH term—for example, when you are not finding what you think ought to be there, or when you are not sure where to look. For example, NEAR DROWNING is a MeSH term, but papers indexed under the broader heading DROWNING might contain information that would be useful to a query pertaining to NEAR DROWNING. The use of a broader MeSH term is especially important if you find a MeSH term that is a relatively new one (see MeSH Vocabulary Changes, page 53). Older literature, indexed before the introduction of the new MeSH term, will be indexed under older, broader MeSH terms.

With some interfaces to MEDLINE (PubMed, for example) narrower (more specific) MeSH terms are automatically included in searches for a broader MeSH terms. Thus, a search for ANGINA

PECTORIS would capture all the papers indexed under ANGINA PECTORIS OR ANGINA PECTORIS, VARIANT OR ANGINA, UNSTABLE OR MICROVASCULAR ANGINA. Likewise, MYOCARDIAL ISCHEMIA would capture all the papers indexed under that MeSH term and those that are more specific than MYOCARDIAL ISCHEMIA. (The relationships among these MeSH terms is shown on page 50.) Other MEDLINE interfaces (some institutional configurations of Ovid MEDLINE, for example) do not include narrower MeSH terms unless the user specifically requests that this be done. Such requests are called "explosions." To search ANGINA PECTORIS and all of its narrower headings, you would "explode" ANGINA PECTORIS. Systems that automatically explode MeSH terms usually have an option for suppressing explosions.

Automatic Term Mapping & MeSH

Entry terms (what you type into the search box in PubMed) are automatically mapped to MeSH vocabulary, if a match can be found. In this way, "high blood pressure" is mapped to HYPERTENSION. The brand drug name Aleve® is automatically mapped to NAPROXEN. "Non-insulin-dependent diabetes" is mapped to DIABETES MEL-LITUS, TYPE 2, as is "adult-onset diabetes." "Diabetic foot ulcer" is mapped to DIABETIC FOOT. Clinical lingo like "statins" or "serms" are mapped to HYDROXYMETHYLGLUTARYL-CoA REDUCTASE INHIBITORS or SELECTIVE ESTROGEN RECEPTOR MODULATORS, respectively. Entry terms can even map to substance names that are not MeSH terms (see Supplementary Concept Records, page 61), provided that the choice of such entry terms has been anticipated by those who manage the MeSH vocabulary.

Often this works quite well, but you will want to spend some time with the Entrez MeSH Database, NLM's MeSH Browser, or other MeSH help tool to make sure you are being precise in naming the concept you are thinking of. Otherwise, you may miss the opportunity to use the MeSH vocabulary that would capture a concept that is essential to your search. For example, unlike the mapping of "high blood pressure" to HYPERTENSION described above, "high cholesterol" is *not* mapped to HYPERCHOLESTEROL-EMIA (abnormally high levels of cholesterol in the blood), but the "cholesterol" part of the entry phrase is mapped to CHOLESTEROL (the principal sterol of all higher animals).

When you type "blood pressure" into the query box in PubMed, your query is mapped to BLOOD PRESSURE, which is one of the many specific aspects of CARDIOVASCULAR PHYSIOLOGY. If you are looking for papers about "high blood pressure," you want HYPERTENSION. HYPERTENSION is a disease MeSH term that encompasses more specific MeSH terms—such as HYPERTENSION, PORTAL or HYPER-TENSION, PULMONARY—and it is distinct from the chemicals and drugs MeSH term ANTIHYPERTENSIVE AGENTS. As John Shaw Billings noted in 1881 (see the quotation that opens this chapter, on page 45), "to find accounts similar to your own rare case you must know what your own case is."

MeSH Vocabulary Changes

Biomedical knowledge is constantly changing. New concepts are discovered, and old ones take on new meanings. Therefore, Medical Subject Headings must change accordingly. At the start of the AIDS epidemic there was no ACQUIRED IMMUNODEFICIENCY SYNDROME, which was introduced in 1983. Articles on this subject that were indexed before 1983 were indexed with the MeSH terms that were most appropriate at that time. The search strategy for ACCIDENTS, TRAFFIC AND TELEPHONE that opens this chapter was constructed in 1999. Since then (in 2003), CELLULAR PHONE has become a MeSH term. Because CELLULAR PHONE is a narrower heading than TELEPHONE, the original search strategy still works in PubMed and other interfaces that automatically "explode" MeSH terms to include more specific MeSH terms. (Searching under TELEPHONE in PubMed gives you TELEPHONE OR ANSWERING SERVICES OR CELLULAR PHONE OR MODEMS.) In fact, at this writing, two years after the introduction of CELLULAR PHONE, the original search strategy remains useful; the many pre-2003 papers concerning cell phones are still indexed under TELEPHONE. When new MeSH terms are introduced, previously indexed articles are *not* usually re-indexed.

Subheadings (Qualifiers)

To make your searches with MeSH terms more precise, you can take advantage of the system of subheadings that the National Library of Medicine has created for them. When the indexers assign a MeSH term to a citation, they often include one or more subheadings that more precisely describe how the MeSH term is being used. For example, a paper about gastrointestinal bleeding caused by ASPIRIN would be indexed with the subheading *adverse effects* applied to ASPIRIN. Such a paper might also be indexed under GASTROINTESTINAL HEMORRHAGE with the subheading *chemically induced* applied to it.

The choice of subheadings that might be applied to a particular MeSH term depends on the MeSH term itself. MeSH terms are classified in broad categories—such as anatomy, organisms, diseases, chemicals and drugs, biological sciences, physical sciences, health care, etc. (Table 3-1)—and each category or branch within that category has its own list of possible subheadings. For example, Table 3-2 lists the subheadings that might be assigned to MeSH terms concerning diseases, and Table 3-3 lists those for chemicals and drugs. Note that some subheadings will not be appropriate to all of the MeSH terms within a category. Use the Entrez MeSH Database or NLM's MeSH Browser to see which subheadings can be applied to which MeSH terms, and to see subheading definitions.

Some interfaces call them "qualifiers" and some call them "subheadings," and the best interfaces will help you find which ones can be applied to the MeSH terms that you want to use for your searches. In most interfaces, subheadings are selected by clicking on their check boxes. In addition, some interfaces allow you to type in subheadings as part of the MeSH term, following the format MeSH term/subheading. For example, "aspirin/adverse effects [mh]" or "aspirin/adverse effects" or "aspirin/ae" entered into PubMed's query box will produce the same result as a search constructed within the Entrez MeSH Database. The MeSH term/subheading combinations that you see in some search result displays (Citation Display in PubMed) have links that can become the basis for a new search. The references that appear in the chapter endnotes in this book provide illustrations of how subheadings are used.

Subheadings are a powerful tool for sharply focusing a search. For example, if you were interested in ASPIRIN only from the standpoint its *economics,* then applying this subheading to it would reduce the number of citations from 4,705 to 57 over the past five years. Or, if your interest in ASPIRIN was from the standpoint of its *pharmacokinetics* (the study of its absorption, metabolism, and excretion), you could use this subheading to reduce the number of citations from 4,705 to 71. Use of the subheading *poisoning* with ASPIRIN narrows the number of citations from 4,705 to 27. Use of the subheading *history* with ASPIRIN narrows the number of citations from 4,705 to 32. Even *therapeutic use,* the subheading most often applied to ASPIRIN, significantly reduces the number of citations, from 4,705 to 3,673. In some instances, you may wish to use more than one subheading. These can be ORed (as is the case when more than one subheading is checked in the Entrez MeSH database), or two MeSH/subheading combinations can be ANDed. As an example of the latter, you could search for papers concerning the *history* of the *therapeutic use* of ASPIRIN. Here is such a search, spanning a much larger time frame than five years, which is appropriate for this query:

❖ The *MeSH index* contained 25,760 citations indexed under ASPIRIN between 1966 and 2004.

❖ Of these, 16,752 were indexed under ASPIRIN with the subheading "therapeutic use" applied to it.

❖ Of these, 37 were also indexed under ASPIRIN with the

TABLE 3–2
Subheadings That Might Be Used within the Diseases (C) Category of MeSH Terms

blood
chemically induced
classification
complications
congenital
diagnosis
diet therapy
drug therapy
economics
embryology
enzymology
epidemiology
ethnology
etiology
genetics
history
immunology
metabolism
microbiology
mortality
nursing
parasitology
pathology
physiopathology
prevention & control
psychology

radiography
radionuclide imaging
radiotherapy
rehabilitation
surgery
therapy
ultrasonography
urine
veterinary
virology

You can type any of these subheadings into the Entrez MeSH Database query box to see how they are defined.

TABLE 3-3
Subheadings That Might Be Used within the Chemicals and Drugs (D) Category of MeSH Terms

administration & dosage
adverse effects
agonists
analysis
analogs & derivatives
antagonists & inhibitors
biosynthesis
blood
cerebrospinal fluid
chemical synthesis
chemistry
classification
contraindications
deficiency
diagnostic use
economics
genetics
history
immunology
isolation & purification
metabolism
pharmacokinetics
pharmacology
physiology
poisoning
radiation effects
secretion
standards
supply & distribution
therapeutic use
toxicity
urine

You can type any of these subheadings into the Entrez MeSH Database query box to see how they are defined.

subheading "history" applied to it.

❖ When these results were narrowed to publications in English, 26 citations were found. One of these was a broadly focused review that was published in *Scientific American* (Weissmann 1991).

Concepts Concerning Pharmacology & Therapeutics

MeSH terms pertaining to the therapeutic use of drugs can be found within most of the categories of Main Headings shown in Table 3-1 on page 47. For example, DRUG INTERACTIONS is within the Biological Sciences Category (G), COST-BENEFIT ANALYSIS is within the Health Care Category (H), and FORMULARIES is within the Information Science Category (L). A MeSH term from the Diseases Category (C), qualified with the "drug therapy" subheading might be a good place to start. However, the Chemicals and Drugs Category (D) deserves special mention, for two reasons. First, it is an especially rich category, containing thousands of MeSH terms. Second, this category of MeSH terms is supplemented by an additional controlled vocabulary called Supplementary Concept Records, which will be discussed in the next section.

First, an overview. Each of the sixteen broad categories of Main Headings shown in Table 3-1 (A through N, V and Z) contains hundreds to thousands of MeSH terms, arranged hierarchically. In most instances, you will use the Entrez MeSH Database or similar tool to see how (or whether) your entry terms correspond to the MeSH terms most appropriate to your needs, without regard for their category. However, another way to find MeSH terms—or at least to deepen your appreciation of the richness of this vocabulary—is to start at the "top" of a category and explore some of its branches. For example, if you enter "diseases category" (with quotes) in the Entrez MeSH Database and follow the link to the full display, you will see the 23 branches of the Diseases Category (C) (beginning with ANIMAL DISEASES and the many branches of these, continuing with BACTERIAL INFECTIONS AND MYCOSES and its many branches, and so on, with each main branch listed alphabetically. Similarly, you can start at the top of the Chemicals and Drugs Category (D) by entering "chemicals and drugs category" (with quotes). Following the link to the full display, you will see its 16 main branches (Table 3-4) and the first tier of branches beneath these. The hyperlinks from any branch can be followed to see more specific (and related) MeSH terms. This can be a time-consuming but illuminating exercise.

The Chemicals and Drugs Category (D) is by far the largest category of MeSH terms. Only the Diseases Category (C) comes close. To give a single example, one of the main branches is CHEMICAL ACTIONS AND USES. Here are some of the branches that show the relation of this MeSH term to ANTIHYPERTENSIVE AGENTS:

All MeSH Categories
  D. Chemicals and Drugs Category
     CHEMICAL ACTIONS AND USES
       PHARMACOLOGIC ACTIONS
         THERAPEUTIC USES
           CARDIOVASCULAR AGENTS
             ANTIHYPERTENSIVE AGENTS

At each level, there is extensive branching, with the same MeSH term sometimes appearing on multiple branches, so the hierarchy of terms is more complex than pictured here. Furthermore, the Chemicals and Drugs Category contains other MeSH terms, besides ANTIHYPERTENSIVE AGENTS, that pertain to the drug treatment of HYPERTENSION. Among these are DIURETICS, as well as CALCIUM CHANNEL BLOCKERS (broader headings, which locate this MeSH term on multiple branches, are CARDIOVASCULAR AGENTS and MOLECULAR MECHANISMS OF ACTION) and ADRENERGIC BETA-ANTAGONISTS (broader is ADRENERGIC ANTAGONISTS) and ANGIOTENSIN-CONVERTING ENZYME INHIBITORS (broader is PROTEASE INHIBITORS), to name of a few.

TABLE 3–4
Main Branches of the Chemicals and Drugs Category (D),
Showing Branches of THERAPEUTIC USES
(+ Indicates Further Branching)
(2006 MeSH)

AMINO ACIDS, PEPTIDES, AND PROTEINS +
BIOLOGICAL FACTORS +
BIOMEDICAL AND DENTAL MATERIALS +
CARBOHYDRATES +
CHEMICAL ACTIONS AND USES +
    PHARMACOLOGIC ACTIONS
        MOLECULAR MECHANISMS OF ACTION +
        PHYSIOLOGICAL EFFECTS OF DRUGS +
        THERAPEUTIC USES
            ANTI-ALLERGIC AGENTS
            ANTI-INFECTIVE AGENTS +
            ANTI-INFLAMMATORY AGENTS +
            ANTILIPEMIC AGENTS +
            ANTINEOPLASTIC AGENTS +
            ANTIRHEUMATIC AGENTS +
            CARDIOVASCULAR AGENTS +
            CENTRAL NERVOUS SYSTEM AGENTS +
            DERMATOLOGIC AGENTS +
            GASTROINTESTINAL AGENTS +
            HEMATOLOGIC AGENTS +
            RENAL AGENTS +
            REPRODUCTIVE CONTROL AGENTS +
            RESPIRATORY SYSTEM AGENTS +
            STIMULANTS (HISTORICAL)
        SPECIALTY USES OF CHEMICALS +
        TOXIC ACTIONS +
COMPLEX MIXTURES +
ENZYMES AND COENZYMES +
HETEROCYCLIC COMPOUNDS +
HORMONES, HORMONE SUBSTITUTES, AND HORMONE ANTAGONISTS +
INORGANIC CHEMICALS +
LIPIDS +
MACROMOLECULAR SUBSTANCES +
NUCLEIC ACIDS, NUCLEOTIDES, AND NUCLEOSIDES +
ORGANIC CHEMICALS +
PHARMACEUTICAL PREPARATIONS +
POLYCYCLIC COMPOUNDS +

Despite the richness of concepts contained within the many Main Headings (Descriptors, MeSH terms) that comprise the Chemicals and Drugs Category of MeSH, the rapid expansion of knowledge about chemicals and proteins requires a correspondingly rapid-changing supplementary vocabulary. Main Headings are updated annually; Supplementary Concept Records, discussed below, are updated on a daily basis.

Supplementary Concept Records (Substance Names)

The many substances that are described in the literature need to be named with a controlled vocabulary. Some of them, like ASPIRIN or LISINOPRIL, are MeSH terms. But most substances are not part of the MeSH trees of inter-related MeSH terms. Instead, these substances are part of a separate controlled vocabulary called "supplementary concepts," which are mainly chemical and protein concepts. Each of these "supplementary concepts" or "substance names" is described in a "Supplementary Concept Record," of which there are more than 150,000. These include the substance name itself, corresponding registry number (from Chemical Abstracts Service or Enzyme Commission Nomenclature number), entry terms (including synonyms, closely related names, trade names, and lab numbers) that map to the substance name, pharmacological action, date of introduction, and related MeSH terms.

Like MeSH terms, substance names can be used for searching. When you find a substance name in the Entrez MeSH Database, it will be marked as such. For example, using "Lipitor" as an entry term, we see "atorvastatin [Substance Name]." Subheadings and other MeSH features are not available within Substance Names.

Pharmacological Action [PA] Category of MeSH

Following a procedure that began in 1996, articles about the action of a drug or chemical are indexed both under the MeSH term for the drug or chemical and that for the pharmacologic action being

studied. Thus, a paper about aspirin's ability to prevent the clump-
ing of platelets would be indexed under both ASPIRIN and PLATE-
LET AGGREGATION INHIBITORS. Similarly, a paper about aspirin's
anti-inflammatory effects would be indexed under both ASPIRIN
and ANTI-INFLAMMATORY AGENTS, NON-STEROIDAL. Likewise,
a paper about simvastatin's ability to block the synthesis of cholesterol by inhibiting the enzyme HMG-CoA reductase would
be indexed both under SIMVASTATIN and HYDROXYMETHYLGLU-
TARYL-CoA REDUCTASE INHIBITORS. In each of these examples,
we see a drug name that is a MeSH term and a particular type of
pharmacologic action. All of the terms mentioned in this paragraph fall under the Chemicals and Drugs Category of MeSH
(see Tables 3-1 and 3-4). If you look in the Entrez MeSH Database or NLM's MeSH Browser for PLATELET AGGREGATION IN-
HIBITORS, or for ANTI-INFLAMMATORY AGENTS, NON-STEROIDAL,
or for HYDROXYMETHYLGLUTARYL-CoA REDUCTASE INHIBITORS,
to see where they fall in the hierarchy of MeSH terms, you will
see that they are usually the last branch. The hierarchy cannot be
used to view a list of all PLATELET AGGREGATION INHIBITORS, or
of any other specific pharmacologic action.

To solve this problem a new MeSH category, *Pharmacological Action [PA]*, was created in 2003. Each *Pharmacological Action*
includes (ORs together) all of the MeSH terms and substance
names thought to share that effect. The criterion for inclusion is
that at least 20 papers have found an association with the particular
pharmacological action. Thus, the Pharmacological Action category
"Platelet Aggregation Inhibitors" includes a long list of substance
names (such as 1,2-benzisothiazoline-3-one) and several MeSH
terms (such as ASPIRIN). When you look in the Entrez MeSH
Database for "statins," you will see two entries for HMG-CoA
reductase inhibitors:

1: Hydroxymethylglutaryl-CoA Reductase Inhibitors
Compounds that inhibit HMG-CoA reductases. They have been
shown to directly lower cholesterol synthesis.

Year introduced: 1998

    2: Hydroxymethylglutaryl-CoA Reductase Inhibitors [Pharmacological Action]

The full display for the first entry looks like that for any MeSH term. The full display for the second entry [Pharmacological Action] is different, in that there are no check boxes for subheadings or for anything else, no placing of the term within the MeSH trees. Instead, we find a list of drugs (both substance names and MeSH terms) that share this pharmacological action. The *Pharmacological Action* entry, which can be sent to the search box for a PubMed search, or is directly searchable in PubMed with the entry tag [PA] or [Pharmacological Action] rather than [MH] or [MeSH], is broader. It captures articles that are indexed under a particular branch of PHARMACOLOGIC ACTIONS, as well as all the substances that have that pharmacologic action. For example, here are two searches for papers about skeletal muscle damage (RHABDOMYOLYSIS) associated with the use of statins:

Search Strategy with MeSH Term:

* ❖ Searching for HYDROXYMETHYLGLUTARYL-CoA REDUCTASE INHIBITORS [MeSH] found 5,520 citations.

* ❖ Limiting these 5,520 citations to articles also indexed under RHABDOMYOLYSIS found 171 citations.

Search Strategy with Pharmacological Action:

* ❖ On the other hand, searching for *hydroxymethylglutaryl-CoA reductase inhibitors* [Pharmacological Action] found 9,795 CITATIONS.

* ❖ Limiting these 9,795 citations to articles also indexed under RHABDOMYOLYSIS found 269 citations.

Which strategy should be used? It depends on what you are trying to accomplish. For most searches, the first search strategy would be most useful. Essentially, it asks, "What articles report on an association between the use of HYDROXYMETHYLGLUTARYL-CoA REDUCTASE INHIBITORS (compounds have been shown to decrease cholesterol synthesis by inhibiting HMG-CoA reductases) and RHABDOMYOLYSIS (necrosis or disintegration of skeletal muscle often followed by myoglobinuria)?" This strategy will capture the main reports on this adverse effect. The second strategy casts a broader net. It ORs together all of the substances with this shared pharmacological action. It captures a case report—missed by the first strategy—of a patient with mild chronic renal failure who developed severe RHABDOMYOLYSIS after combined exposure to SIMVASTATIN and COLCHICINE (Baker 2004). The second strategy increases recall (pages 33-34). It says, "Many substances are hydroxymethylglutaryl-CoA reductase inhibitors. Show me all the articles that associate the use of any of these substances with RHABDOMYOLYSIS."

MeSH vs. Major MeSH

When the indexers at the National Library of Medicine assign the dozen or so MeSH terms that characterize the concepts contained in articles, they identify a few of them as central concepts. (See for example, the starred entries on pages 27-28.) These *Major MeSH* entries for each article are the same as those that appeared in the printed *Index Medicus*—until the end of 2004, when its publication ceased, having been fully eclipsed by the free world-wide availability of more complete, current, and easily searched Web versions. Remember (from Chapter 1), a printed index must limit the number of subject headings used to characterize each article; otherwise, it would become much too large. Therefore, only the MeSH terms of major importance to an article ended up in the printed *Index Medicus*. MEDLINE can be searched by designating a MeSH term as being one of these "Major Topic headings" or "Major MeSH." The MeSH term itself is the same, but the search strategy takes advantage of the context in which the MeSH term was applied during indexing. For example, when a search for IBUPROFEN was restricted to its use as a Major Topic heading, 2,472 citations were found, compared with 4,010 without this special contextual limit. Similarly, a search for review articles (a Publication Type limit) about IBUPROFEN, with its use restricted to Major Topic heading, found 71 articles, compared with 185 without this restriction.

This feature can be helpful, but it should be used with some caution: A lot of valuable information about IBUPROFEN is contained in articles that don't treat IBUPROFEN as their "Major Topic." For example, a study that attempted to answer the question of whether or not non-steroidal anti-inflammatory drugs like IBUPROFEN might impair the cardioprotective effects of ASPIRIN would have been missed by a search that characterized IBUPROFEN as a "Major Topic" (Garcia Rodriguez 2004). This paper was indexed under ASPIRIN AND IBUPROFEN, along with many other MeSH terms. Among these, ANTI-INFLAMMATORY AGENTS, NON-STEROIDAL and CYCLOOXYGENASE INHIBITORS were each characterized as being a "Major Topic."

Age Groups

Publications that involve humans are assigned special Medical Subject Headings that indicate the age range(s) of the subjects involved. These are useful for focusing your search results. For example, considerations for the treatment of ASTHMA in an 85-year-old might differ from those in a 15-year-old. In some MEDLINE interfaces, age-specific Medical Subject Headings cannot be used to initiate a search; they can only be used to limit searches. In some interfaces to MEDLINE, age limit selection options appear on the main search screen, along with language, publication type, and other limits. These age group Medical Subject Headings (with their age ranges in parentheses) are:

INFANT, NEWBORN (birth–1 month)
INFANT (1–23 months)
All Infant (birth–23 months) (INFANT, NEWBORN OR INFANT)

CHILD, PRESCHOOL (2–5 years)

CHILD (6–12 years)

ADOLESCENT (13–18 years)

All Child (0–18 years) (combines age-specific MeSH terms)

All Adult (19+ years) (combines age-specific MeSH terms)

ADULT (19–44 years)

MIDDLE AGED (45–64 years)

AGED (65+ years)

AGED, 80 AND OVER (80+ years)

In addition, there are a number of more specialized age-related MeSH terms that pertain to particular concerns among age groups, such as INFANT NUTRITION, SUDDEN INFANT DEATH, HOMELESS YOUTH, MATERNAL AGE, ELDER ABUSE, HEALTH SERVICES FOR THE AGED, FRAIL ELDERLY, etc.

Geographical Locations

Specific Medical Subject Headings are available for many places— for countries, regions of the UNITED STATES, states, or cities. These too can be helpful in searching. For example, if you were interested in HYPERTENSION among persons living in CHICAGO, you might want to see whether this particular health problem had ever been the subject of a study that involved this particular location.

Sources of MeSH Information

The National Library of Medicine maintains a MeSH web site (home of the NLM MeSH Browser Home-page) and a variety of other MeSH resources; see Appendix A.

PubMed contains a link to the Entrez MeSH Database, from which you can construct your search strategies. Several animated tutorials are available from within this database. Entry terms are mapped to likely MeSH terms, displayed in a summary format. Each of these MeSH terms can be viewed in a full display that shows its definition, allowable subheadings (as check boxes), entry terms (the terms that automatically map to it), its place within the hierarchy of related MeSH terms, the year that it was introduced, and other information. The Entrez MeSH Database is an excellent tool!

The MeSH terms that are used in this book represent a tiny fraction of those that are available. Together, these 23,880 MeSH terms can be thought of as a vocabulary for characterizing all biomedical knowledge. Take the time to see how the concepts you are working with have been named. Spend some time with the Entrez MeSH Database and other MeSH tools. Do text word searches in PubMed and follow the "Details" link to see how your queries were interpreted. Examine the MeSH terms that have been applied to articles that interest you. Links from these can be followed for more information or used as the basis for a new search.

Until 2003, the National Library of Medicine published three annual reference books: *Medical Subject Headings: Annotated Alphabetic List* (detailed information about Medical Subject Headings), *Permuted Medical Subject Headings* (a way to find out which one to use when you were not sure where to look in the alphabetic list), and *Medical Subject Headings: Tree Structures* (as illustrated on pages 48-51, Medical Subject Headings are hierarchically related to one another; the tree structures describe those relationships). These were discontinued, because most searchers are now accustomed to using online MeSH tools, which are constantly updated. Still in print, however, is *Medical Subject Headings* (formerly called *MeSH, Supplement to the Index Medicus* when the *Index Medicus* was still being printed). This book, which is commonly called the "Black and White MeSH," in reference to its cover design, combines the alphabetic arrangement and tree structures within a single publication and provides a primer on MeSH. Although they are out of date (MeSH are continually updated), these books will be available at your medical library, and, if they are nearby, you might find them to be a handy means for orienting yourself to this important topic.

As you might expect, MEDLINE itself is a useful resource for finding articles about MeSH. Many of these are research articles that are aimed at informatics researchers (Haynes, McKibbon et al 2005), but some are more broadly focused (Gore 2003; Coletti and Bleich 2001; Lowe and Barnett 1994) , and others are aimed at specific disciplines (Kahn and Ninomiya 2003). MEDICAL SUBJECT HEADINGS was introduced as a MeSH term in 2005, while this chapter was being written:

All Categories of Medical Subject Headings
   L. Information Science Category
       INFORMATION SCIENCE
        INFORMATION SERVICES
         DOCUMENTATION
          VOCABULARY, CONTROLLED
           SUBJECT HEADINGS
            MEDICAL SUBJECT HEADINGS

Older papers on this subject are indexed under SUBJECT HEADINGS AND MEDLINE (or, in some cases since 2003, SUBJECT HEADINGS AND PUBMED). PUBMED is broader than MEDLINE, so it can be used to capture older papers when searching with interfaces that automatically explode MeSH terms. Such explosions of PUBMED result in searches for PUBMED OR MEDLINE. Be careful not to search under "mesh" without qualifications: otherwise you will get SURGICAL MESH, as well as MEDICAL SUBJECT HEADINGS, MEDLINE, at least two substance names, and "mesh" as a text word.

References

Baker SK, Goodwin S, Sur M, Tarnopolsky MA (2004). Cytoskeletal myotoxicity from simvastatin and colchicine. *Muscle Nerve.* 2004 Dec;30(6):799-802. **MeSH Terms:** aged; *COLCHICINE (subheading: adverse effects); *CYTOSKELETON (subheadings: drug effects, pathology); HUMANS; MALE; MUSCULAR DISEASES (subheadings: chemically induced; pathology); RHABDOMYOLYSIS (subheadings: chemically induced; pathology); *SIMVASTATIN (subheading: adverse effects); **Publication Type:** case reports. PMID: 15389652

Billings JS ([1881] 1965). *Our Medical Literature. Selected Papers. Compiled, with a Life of Billings,* by Frank Bradway Rogers. Chicago, Medical Library Association: 129-130.

Chapman S, Schofield WN (1998). "Lifesavers and Samaritans: emergency use of cellular (mobile) phones in Australia." *Accid Anal Prev* 30(6): 815-9. **MeSH Terms:** ACCIDENTS, TRAFFIC (subheadings: prevention & control; statistics & numerical data); AUSTRALIA; *EMERGENCIES; *HELPING BEHAVIOR; HUMAN; SAMPLING STUDIES; SUPPORT, NON-U.S. GOV'T; *TELEPHONE (subheading: utilization); **Publication Type:** journal article. PMID: 9805524

Clarke M, Greaves L, et al (1997). MeSH terms must be used in Medline searches. *BMJ* 314(7088): 1203. **MeSH Terms:** INFORMATION STOR-AGE AND RETRIEVAL; MEDLINE; SUBJECT HEADINGS; UNITED STATES; **Publication Type:** letter; comment. PMID: 9146422

Coletti MH and Bleich HL (2001). Medical subject headings used to search the biomedical literature. *J Am Med Inform Assoc.* 2001 Jul-Aug;8(4):317-23. **MeSH Terms:** ABSTRACTING AND INDEXING (subheading: history); HISTORY, 19TH CENTURY; HISTORY, 20TH CENTURY; *INFORMATION STORAGE AND RETRIEVAL (subheadings: history; methods); INTERNET; *MEDLARS (subheading: history); *MEDLINE (subheading: history); *SUBJECT HEADINGS; VOCABULARY, CONTROLLED; **Publication Type:** historical article; journal article. PMID: 11418538

Garcia Rodriguez LA, Varas-Lorenzo C, et al (2004). Nonsteroidal antiinflammatory drugs and the risk of myocardial infarction in the general population. *Circulation.* 2004 Jun 22;109(24):3000-6. **MeSH Terms:** AGED; AGED, 80 AND OVER; *ANTI-INFLAMMATORY AGENTS, NON-STEROIDAL (subheadings: pharmacology; therapeutic use); ASPIRIN (subheadings: administration & dosage; pharmacology; therapeutic use); *CARDIOTONIC AGENTS (subheadings: administration & dosage; pharmacology; therapeutic use); CASE-CONTROL STUDIES; COHORT STUDIES; COMORBIDITY; CORONARY DISEASE (subheadings: drug therapy; mortality); *CYCLOOXYGENASE INHIBITORS (subhead-ings: administration & dosage; adverse effects; pharmacology; thera-peutic use); DICLOFENAC (subheadings: pharmacology; therapeutic use); DOSE-RESPONSE RELATIONSHIP, DRUG; DRUG SYNERGISM; DRUG UTILIZATION; FEMALE; FOLLOW-UP STUDIES; HUMANS; IBUPROFEN (subheadings: administration & dosage; pharmacology; therapeutic use); LACTONES (subheading: adverse effects); MALE; MIDDLE AGED; *MYOCARDIAL INFARCTION (subheadings: chemically induced; epidemiology; prevention & control); NAPROXEN (subheadings: pharmacology; therapeutic use); ODDS RATIO; RESEARCH SUPPORT, NON-U.S. GOV'T; RISK FACTORS; SPAIN (subheading: epidemiology; **Publication Type:** journal article. PMID: 15197149

Gore G (2003). Searching the medical literature. *Inj Prev* 9(2):103-4. **MeSH Terms:** *DATABASES, BIBLIOGRAPHIC; INFORMATION SERVICES; *INFORMATION STORAGE AND RETRIEVAL (subheading: methods); MEDLINE; ONLINE SYSTEMS; SUBJECT HEADINGS. **Publication Type:** journal article. PMID: 12810733

Haynes RB, McKibbon et al (2005). Optimal search strategies for retrieving scientifically strong studies of treatment from Medline: analytical survey. *BMJ* 330(7501):1179. **MeSH Terms:** *INFORMATION STORAGE AND RETRIEVAL (subheading: standards); *MEDLINE; *MEDICAL SUBJECT HEADINGS; RESEARCH SUPPORT, N.I.H., EXTRAMURAL; RESEARCH SUPPORT, U.S. Gov'T, P.H.S. **Publication Type:** journal article. PMID: 15894554

Iglesia CB, Fenner DE, et al (1997). The use of mesh in gynecologic surgery. *Int Urogynecol J Pelvic Floor Dysfunct* 8(2): 105-15. **MeSH Terms:** FEMALE; *GENITAL DISEASES, FEMALE (subheading: surgery); HUMAN; MATERIALS TESTING; POLYETHYLENE TEREPHTHALATES (subheading: therapeutic use); POLYGLYCOLIC ACID (subheading: therapeutic use); *POLYTETRAFLUOROETHYLENE (subheading: therapeutic use); SURGICAL MESH; UROLOGIC DISEASES (subheading: surgery); **Publication Type:** journal article; review; review, tutorial. PMID: 9297599

Kahn TJ, Ninomiya H (2003). Changing vocabularies: a guide to help bioethics searchers find relevant literature in National Library of Medicine databases using the Medical Subject Headings (MeSH) indexing vocabulary. *Kennedy Inst Ethics J* 13(3):275-311. **MeSH Terms:** *ABSTRACTING AND INDEXING; *BIOETHICS; CATALOGS, LIBRARY; *DATABASES, BIBLIOGRAPHIC; *INFORMATION STORAGE AND RETRIEVAL (subheading: methods); LITERATURE; *MEDLINE; NATIONAL LIBRARY OF MEDICINE (U.S.); *PUBMED; *SUBJECT HEADINGS; UNITED

STATES; **Publication Type:** journal article. PMID: 14577461

Levine M, Walter S, et al (1994). Users' guides to the medical literature. IV. How to use an article about harm. Evidence-Based Medicine Working Group. *JAMA* 271(20): 1615-9. **MeSH Terms:** GUIDELINES; MEDICAL INFORMATICS APPLICATIONS; *MEDLINE; *OUTCOME ASSESSMENT (HEALTH CARE) (subheading: standards); *PATIENT CARE PLANNING (subheading: standards); *PERIODICALS; PHYSICIAN'S PRACTICE PATTERNS (subheading: standards); REPRODUCIBILITY OF RESULTS; *SUBJECT HEADINGS; TECHNOLOGY, MEDICAL; TREATMENT OUTCOME; **Publication Type:** journal article. PMID: 8182815

Lowe HJ, Barnett BO (1994). Understanding and using the medical subject headings (MeSH) vocabulary to perform literature searches. *JAMA* 271(14): 1103-8. **MeSH Terms:** DATABASES, BIBLIOGRAPHIC; INFORMATION STORAGE AND RETRIEVAL; MEDICAL INFORMATICS (subheading: methods); MEDLARS; MEDLINE (subheading: organization & administration); NATIONAL LIBRARY OF MEDICINE (U.S.); SUBJECT HEADINGS; UNITED STATES; **Publication Type:** journal article. PMID: 8151853

Maclure M, Mittleman MA (1997). Cautions about car telephones and collisions. *N Engl J Med* 336(7): 501-2. **MeSH Terms:** *ACCIDENTS, TRAFFIC; AUTOMOBILE DRIVING (subheading: legislation & jurisprudence); CASE-CONTROL STUDIES; RISK; *TELEPHONE (subheading: legislation & jurisprudence); **Publication Type:** comment; editorial. PMID: 9017945

McKibbon KA, Haynes, RB et al (1990). "How good are clinical MEDLINE searches? A comparative study of clinical end-user and librarian searches." *Comput Biomed Res* 23(6): 583-93. **MeSH Terms:** EVALUATION STUDIES; GRATEFUL MED; *MEDLINE; REPRODUCIBILITY OF RESULTS; SUBJECT HEADINGS; SUPPORT, NON-U.S. GOV'T; SUPPORT, U.S. GOV'T, P.H.S.; USER-COMPUTER INTERFACE; **Publication Type:** journal article. PMID: 2276266

Redelmeier DA, Tibshirani RJ (1997). Association between cellular-telephone calls and motor vehicle collisions. *N Engl J Med* 336(7): 453-8. **MeSH Terms:** *ACCIDENTS, TRAFFIC (subheadings: prevention & control; statistics & numerical data); ADULT; AUTOMOBILE DRIVING (subheading: legislation & jurisprudence); CASE-CONTROL STUDIES;

FEMALE; HUMAN; MALE; MIDDLE AGE; ONTARIO; RISK; SAFETY; SUPPORT, NON-U.S. GOV'T; *TELEPHONE (subheadings: legislation & jurisprudence; statistics & numerical data); **Publication Type:** journal article. PMID: 9017937

Tseng AL, Foisy MM (1997). Management of drug interactions in patients with HIV. *Ann Pharmacother* 31(9): 1040-58. **MeSH Terms:** DRUG INTERACTIONS; *DRUG THERAPY (subheading: adverse effects); HUMAN; *HIV INFECTIONS (subheadings: drug therapy; metabolism); **Publication Type:** journal article; review; review, tutorial. PMID: 9296246

Violanti JM (1998). Cellular phones and fatal traffic collisions. *Accid Anal Prev* 30(4): 519-24. **MeSH Terms:** *ACCIDENTS, TRAFFIC; ADULT; CASE-CONTROL STUDIES; CONFIDENCE INTERVALS; FEMALE; HUMAN; LOGISTIC MODELS; MALE; MIDDLE AGE; ODDS RATIO; *TELEPHONE; **Publication Type:** journal article. PMID: 9666247

Weissmann G (1991). Aspirin. *Sci Am* 264(1): 84-90. **MeSH Terms:** ANALGESIA; ANTI-INFLAMMATORY AGENTS, NON-STEROIDAL (subheadings: pharmacology; therapeutic use); ASPIRIN (subheadings: administration & dosage; adverse effects; history; pharmacology; therapeutic use); BLOOD COAGULATION DISORDERS (subheading: chemically induced); CELL MEMBRANE (subheading: drug effects); CEREBROVASCULAR DISORDERS (subheading: prevention & control); COMPARATIVE STUDY; DRUG INDUSTRY; HEART DISEASES (subheading: prevention & control); HISTORY OF MEDICINE, 18TH CENTURY; HISTORY OF MEDICINE, 19TH CENTURY; HISTORY OF MEDICINE, 20TH CENTURY; HUMANS; INFLAMMATION (subheading: drug therapy); PLANT EXTRACTS; PROSTAGLANDINS (subheading: physiology); STOMACH DISEASES (subheading: chemically induced); TREES; **Substances:** anti-inflammatory agents, non-steroidal; cyclooxygenase inhibitors; plant extracts; prostaglandins; aspirin; **Publication Type:** historical article. PMID: 1899486

4

Publication Types and
Other Limiting Strategies

W E often begin searching from a point of relative ignorance, unable to anticipate the intersection of MeSH terms and Text Words that will produce the most useful list of citations. MEDLINE is infinitely flexible, and several iterations of a search are often required. This chapter illustrates how to address the problem of sorting out the varying kinds of information that are produced by a search. Accordingly, it is organized by Publication Type, focusing on those that are most commonly used.

Publication Types are another means by which the indexers at the National Library of Medicine characterize each citation before it is entered into MEDLINE. *Unlike MeSH terms, Subheadings, and Supplementary Concepts, which describe the subject content of a citation, Publication Types describe the manner in which this subject content is conveyed or how it was studied*—as a letter, an editorial, or a clinical trial, for example. Some interfaces offer a pull-down menu choice of a half-dozen or so of the Publication Types that are most often used to limit a search. In PubMed, this is one of the Limits options. In addition, citations can be displayed in formats that contain links from the Publication Type(s). These links can be followed to learn more, or to modify your search strategy. Table 4-1 provides a sampling of Publication Types. Each of these is searchable in MEDLINE. Like other MeSH, their organization is hierarchical (see Chapter 3).

Practice Guideline

Articles that have been characterized as being a "practice guideline" exist for a wide array of clinical interventions. Practice guidelines that have been promulgated by an authoritative body, such as the American Diabetes Association or the National Institutes of Health (NIH) are particularly valuable. For example, when the NIH's National Heart Lung and Blood Institute published their highly-regarded *Seventh Report of the Joint National Committee on Prevention, Detection, Evaluation, and Treatment of High Blood Pressure* (Chobanian 2003), they published the report both as a government publication (freely available at the National Heart Lung and Blood Institute's Web site) and as a 46-page paper in the journal *Hypertension* (also freely available from the journal's Web site). Here is a search strategy that found the journal citation for this important practice guideline:

* ❖ Searching with the MeSH term HYPERTENSION attracted 19,278 English language citations listed during the past five years.

* ❖ Limiting these 19,278 citations to those that were indexed as being of the Publication Type "practice guideline" produced 80 citations, one of which was the *Seventh Report of the Joint National Committee on Prevention, Detection, Evaluation, and Treatment of High Blood Pressure* (Chobanian 2003), which contains a free link to the full text version, both in html and pdf. This strategy also finds an adaptation of this practice guideline for dentists (Herman 2003), the British Hypertension Society's practice guideline (Williams 2004), and others.

Distinction Between MeSH Terms and Publication Types with Similar-Looking Names. Don't confuse the Publication Type "practice guideline" with the MeSH term PRACTICE GUIDELINES

TABLE 4-1
Sampling of Publication Types [PT]

For more information, look in the Entrez MeSH Database. The + sign indicates further branching.

Publication Components+

Publication Formats+
  Classical Article
  Comment
  Editorial
  Guideline
    Practice Guideline
  Historical Article+
  Journal Article
  Legal Cases
  Letter
  News
  Popular Works+
    Patient Education Handout
  Published Erratum
  Review

Study Characteristics
Case Reports
Clinical Conference
Clinical Trial
  Clinical Trial, Phase I
  Clinical Trial, Phase II
  Clinical Trial, Phase III
  Clinical Trial, Phase IV
  Controlled Clinical Trial
  Multicenter Study
  Randomized Controlled
    Trial
Comparative Study
Consensus Development
  Conference+
Evaluation Studies
In Vitro
Meta-Analysis
Multicenter Study
Scientific Integrity Review
Twin Study
Validation Studies

(note the spelling difference—the "s" on the end). The MeSH term PRACTICE GUIDELINES can be used to find papers *about* a published practice guideline, or the development of one. A similar source of confusion might arise in distinguishing between the Publication Type "clinical trial" and CLINICAL TRIALS, or the Publication Type "meta-analysis" and META-ANALYSIS.

Although the MeSH term PRACTICE GUIDELINES will not lead you directly to an actual practice guideline, it can be quite useful in finding information about the creation or impact of one. For example, a search for PRACTICE GUIDELINES AND HYPERTENSION will point you to a prominent clinician's commentary on the *Seventh Report of the Joint National Committee on Prevention, Detection, Evaluation, and Treatment of High Blood Pressure* (Kaplan 2004), studies that evaluated how well it is actually being applied (Steinman 2004; Borzecki 2003), the economic implications of such an EVIDENCE-BASED MEDICINE approach (Fischer and Avorn 2004), and its impact on DRUG UTILIZATION (Fretheim 2003; Nordmann 2003).

In an ideal world, a practice guideline, based on a thorough review of the best published evidence and recently updated by an authoritative committee, would be available for all medical problems. Unfortunately, this is not the case. You might find that the practice guideline you had hoped to find simply does not exist, or what you do find is insufficient; the information you need must be found in other Publication Types.

Clinical Trial, Randomized Controlled Trial, and Multicenter Study

Scientific knowledge about the efficacy and safety of therapeutic interventions comes from a variety of sources—laboratory studies, animal studies, case reports, population-based studies, and clinical trials. Much of this literature concerns drug therapy, the focus of the following comments.

Carefully designed studies in humans will have the greatest

bearing on decisions about medication selection and use, and these can be located by limiting the Publication Type to "clinical trial," "randomized controlled trial," or any of several Publication Types related to clinical trials (see Table 4-1). Of these, "clinical trial" is the most general Publication Type. Each of the phases of clinical trials required for approval by the Food and Drug Administration can be searched as a discrete Publication Type: "clinical trial, phase I" (to establish safety), "clinical trial, phase II" (to establish therapeutic efficacy, dose range, kinetics, and metabolism), and "clinical trial, phase III" (to establish safety and efficacy). Even post-marketing surveillance, "clinical trial, phase IV" (to detect adverse drug reactions, patterns of drug utilization, and additional information), can be searched as a Publication Type, though these are relatively few in number. A "controlled clinical trial" involves the use of a control group, and if assignment to the test and control groups is truly random (e.g., by a random-numbers table), then it is a "randomized controlled trial."

Randomized Controlled Trial. The "randomized controlled trial" is the highest standard for scientific knowledge about the effects of drugs in humans. For example, the drug METFORMIN lowers serum glucose levels by increasing insulin action in peripheral tissues and reducing hepatic glucose output. Here is a search that addressed the question, "What randomized controlled trials have evaluated the effects of METFORMIN in patients with type 2 diabetes (DIABETES MELLITUS, TYPE 2)?":

- ❖ Searching for METFORMIN AND DIABETES MELLITUS, TYPE 2 (both as MeSH terms) found 512 citations during the past five years.

- ❖ Of these, 109 were indexed in the *Publication Type index* as being a "randomized controlled trial."

Multicenter Study. One of the problems in designing any clinical trial is enrolling enough patients. All things considered, bigger is usually better. Some of the largest clinical trials involve patients from several institutions, and each of these clinical trials are characterized as being the Publication Type "multicenter study." When the above search was modified with an additional step, further limiting the 109 randomized controlled trials to those that were also indexed as being a Publication Type "multicenter study," 44 citations were found. Among the results were several reports from the United Kingdom Prospective Diabetes Study Group (Davis 2001). Large randomized multicenter studies such as these are frequently cited as the scientific basis for current knowledge.

Review

If you don't know a lot about a subject, and no guidelines are available, a paper that is indexed as being Publication Type "review" is a good place to start. Review papers are a staple of the medical literature and can be quite valuable in placing more specific papers within a larger context. Review papers can identify issues of controversy, thereby framing questions that can be pursued later in more specific searches. In addition, controversial issues themselves are often the subject of review papers.

When searching for reviews about commonly occurring diseases, you will need to use additional limiting strategies—such as one or more additional MeSH terms, searching for one of the MeSH terms as a Major Topic, applying subheadings, or limiting the results to a particular journal or subset of journals—to avoid too long a list of results.

When I needed to quickly review the topic of OBESITY, from a public health standpoint, here is how I found two papers from a journal that was in my office:

❖ Searching under OBESITY as Major Topic found 39,409 citations.

❖ Limiting these 39,409 citations to those that were also indexed as being Publication Type "review" reduced the number to 4,780.

❖ Further limiting these 4,780 papers to those that were published in the *American Journal of Public Health* found 3 articles. Two of these, from the same issue, were from the Centers for Disease Control and Prevention—an estimate of attributable mortality from obesity in the United States (Flegal 2004) and a broader perspective on addressing the obesity epidemic (Gerberding and Marks 2004).

Here is a search for review papers concerning BREAST NEOPLASMS AND HORMONE REPLACEMENT THERAPY:

❖ Searching for BREAST NEOPLASMS AND HORMONE REPLACEMENT THERAPY as MeSH terms found 1,562 citations.

❖ Limiting these 1,562 citations to those that were also indexed as being Publication Type "review" papers reduced the number to 557.

❖ Further limiting these 557 papers to those that were published a particular subset of journals—the Core Clinical Journals (listed in Appendix B)—reduced the number to 84.

Meta-Analysis

Although review papers are useful, you may want to see the primary literature in all its complexity. As you analyze this literature, you will sometimes find controversies. "Meta-analysis," which is a quantitative technique for pooling the results of many studies and re-analyzing the results, is also a Publication Type. It is one way to approach a controversial issue that has not yet been resolved by a single study of sufficient power. There are relatively few meta-analyses, compared to reviews, so they are fairly easy to find.

For example, let us say that after reading some review papers concerning risk factors for breast cancer, the literature on ALCOHOL DRINKING AND BREAST NEOPLASMS becomes the focus of a careful literature analysis. Although light consumption of alcoholic beverages does not appear to be a risk for breast cancer (Zhang, Kreger et al 1999), there are many studies suggesting that moderate to heavy consumption does pose a risk. How can this evidence be assessed? One meta-analysis, which was a pooled analysis of six prospective studies, found that women consuming 2-5 drinks a day had a 40% higher risk of breast cancer, compared with non-drinkers (Smith-Warner, Spiegelman et al 1998). Another meta-analysis, which included 58,515 women with invasive breast cancer and 95,067 controls from 53 studies, found a similar effect (Hamajima et al 2002). Another meta-analysis found that the risk associated with one drink per day is small (Ellison, Zhang et al 2001). Here is how these meta-analyses were found:

❖ Searching for ALCOHOL DRINKING AND BREAST NEO-PLASMS as MeSH terms attracted 374 citations.

❖ When these were limited to citations those that were indexed as being Publication Type "meta-analysis," 8 citations were found, including the three above-cited articles.

There is also a MeSH term META-ANALYSIS, which is used for articles about this quantitative method.

Systematic Reviews

A meta-analysis provides the quantitative information that is often lacking in traditional narrative reviews, but EVIDENCE-BASED MEDICINE depends on literature that has been reviewed with a focus on methodological quality. Systematic reviews are attempts at synthesizing the best evidence for clinical decisions, making use of both meta-analyses and review articles but paying careful attention to methodology. Examples of systematic reviews are those contained in the Cochrane Database of Systematic Reviews

(Cochrane Reviews) and the Database of Abstracts of Reviews of Effects (DARE). Systematic reviews are not a Publication Type, but they have been indexed as a susbset of MEDLINE, searchable with the addition of "AND systematic [sb]" to a query. PubMed's Clinical Queries page offers a convenient means for using this subset. The systematic reviews subset makes use of the meta-analysis and review Publication Types but refines the search with additional search terms. These search strategies have been carefully evaluated (Shojania and Bero 2001; Montori, Wilcynski, et al 2005).

Editorial

Editorials provide some of the most interesting reading in the medical literature. They are usually thoughtful appraisals of issues of import, often written by individuals who are deeply informed about the issues at hand. You will, of course, find editorials without seeking them, because they will be included in the results from broader searches. Nevertheless, they can be the subject of a specific search. For example, when the last step of the above search strategy for BREAST NEOPLASMS AND ALCOHOL DRINKING was modified, searching instead for the Publication Type "editorial" —rather than "meta-analysis"—nine editorials were found. In one of them, published in the journal *Epidemiology* and entitled "Sobering Data on Alcohol and Breast Cancer," Harvard researchers Walter Willett and Meir Stampfer review the epidemiologic literature, evaluate its criticisms, and note that alcohol appears to increase endogenous estrogen levels (a plausible biological mechanism for increasing breast cancer risk). They acknowledge that the risk is modest but point out that the same might be said about the lack of regular mammography. Noting that few women are aware of the potential risk, they even provide a preliminary draft of a consumer message about the breast cancer risk associated with drinking:

> Consuming more than one drink per day increases the risk of breast cancer to an extent sufficient to negate the benefits of mammogra-

phy. One drink per day probably increases breast cancer to a small degree, but several drinks per week is likely to have a negligible effect. Consuming one or two drinks per day also lowers the risk of heart disease and for many women the benefits may outweigh the risks. Nevertheless, we know of many ways to reduce the risk of heart disease, but few ways to lower breast cancer risk (Willett and Stampfer 1997). *[Reprinted with permissions.]*

Again, editorials provide some of the most interesting reading in the medical literature. Don't ignore them.

References

(1998). United Kingdom Prospective Diabetes Study 24: a 6-year, randomized, controlled trial comparing sulfonylurea, insulin, and metformin therapy in patients with newly diagnosed type 2 diabetes that could not be controlled with diet therapy. United Kingdom Prospective Diabetes Study Group. *Ann Intern Med* 128(3): 165-75. **MeSH Terms:** ADULT; AGED; BLOOD GLUCOSE (subheading: metabolism); COMBINED MODALITY THERAPY; COMPARATIVE STUDY; *DIABETES MELLITUS, NON-INSULIN-DEPENDENT (subheadings: blood; complications; diet therapy; drug therapy); FEMALE; FOLLOW-UP STUDIES; GREAT BRITAIN; HEMOGLOBIN A, GLYCOSYLATED (subheading: metabolism); HUMAN; HYPOGLYCEMIA (subheading: etiology); *HYPOGLYCEMIC AGENTS (subheading: therapeutic use); *INSULIN (subheading: therapeutic use); MALE; *METFORMIN (subheading: therapeutic use); MIDDLE AGE; OBESITY (subheadings: blood; complications); PROSPECTIVE STUDIES; STATISTICS; *SULFONYLUREA COMPOUNDS (subheading: therapeutic use); SUPPORT, NON-U.S. GOV'T; SUPPORT, U.S. GOV'T, P.H.S.; **Publication Type:** clinical trial; journal article; multicenter study; randomized controlled trial. PMID: 9454524

Borzecki AM, Wong AT, et al (2003). Hypertension control: how well are we doing? *Arch Intern Med.* 2003 Dec 8-22;163(22):2705-11. **MeSH Terms:** AGED; *ANTIHYPERTENSIVE AGENTS (subheading: administration & dosage); DIABETES COMPLICATIONS; DIABETIC ANGIOPATHIES (subheading: prevention & control); FEMALE; GUIDELINE ADHERENCE; HUMANS; *HYPERTENSION (subheadings: complications; prevention & control); KIDNEY DISEASES (subheading: complications); MALE;

MIDDLE AGED; PRACTICE GUIDELINES; RESEARCH SUPPORT, U.S. GOV'T, NON-P.H.S.; TIME FACTORS; UNITED STATES; VETERANS; **Publication Type:** journal article. PMID: 14662624

Chobanian AV, Bakris GL, et al (2003). Seventh report of the Joint National Committee on Prevention, Detection, Evaluation, and Treatment of High Blood Pressure. *Hypertension.* 2003 Dec;42(6):1206-52. **MeSH Terms:** ADULT; AGED; ANTIHYPERTENSIVE AGENTS (subheading: therapeutic use); BLOOD PRESSURE (subheading: drug effects); BLOOD PRESSURE DETERMINATION (subheadings: methods; standards); CARDIOVASCULAR DISEASES (subheadings: epidemiology; mortality); FEMALE; HUMANS; *HYPERTENSION (subheadings: diagnosis; prevention & control; therapy); MALE; MIDDLE AGED; RESEARCH SUPPORT, U.S. Gov'T, P.H.S.; RISK FACTORS; **Publication Type:** guideline; journal article; practice guideline. PMID: 14656957

Davis TM, Cull CA, et al (2001). Relationship between ethnicity and glycemic control, lipid profiles, and blood pressure during the first 9 years of type 2 diabetes: U.K. Prospective Diabetes Study (UKPDS 55). *Diabetes Care.* 2001 Jul;24(7):1167-74. **MeSH Terms:** *BLOOD GLUCOSE (subheading: metabolism); *BLOOD PRESSURE (subheading: physiology); BODY MASS INDEX; CHOLESTEROL (subheading: blood); COMPARATIVE STUDY; CROSS-SECTIONAL STUDIES; *DIABETES MELLITUS, TYPE 2 (subheadings: blood; genetics; physiopathology; therapy); DIABETIC DIET; *ETHNIC GROUPS; FEMALE; FOLLOW-UP STUDIES; GREAT BRITAIN; HEMOGLOBIN A, GLYCOSYLATED (subheading: analysis); HUMANS; HYPERTENSION (subheading: epidemiology); HYPOGLYCEMIC AGENTS (subheading: therapeutic use); *LIPIDS (subheading: blood); LIPOPROTEINS, HDL CHOLESTEROL (subheading: blood); LIPOPROTEINS, LDL CHOLESTEROL (subheading: blood); MALE; METFORMIN (subheading: therapeutic use); MIDDLE AGED; RESEARCH SUPPORT, NON-U.S. GOV'T; RESEARCH SUPPORT, U.S. GOV'T, P.H.S.; SULFONYLUREA COMPOUNDS (subheading: therapeutic use); TIME FACTORS; TRIGLYCERIDES (subheading: blood); **Publication Type:** clinical trial; journal article; multicenter study; randomized controlled trial. PMID: 11423497

Ellison RC, Zhang Y, et al (2001). *Am J Epidemiol.* 2001 Oct 15;154(8):740-7. **MeSH Terms:** *ALCOHOL DRINKING (subheading: adverse effects); *BREAST NEOPLASMS (subheadings: epidemiology; etiology); CASE-CONTROL STUDIES; COHORT STUDIES; FEMALE; FOL-

LOW-UP STUDIES; HUMANS; RESEARCH SUPPORT, NON-U.S. GOV'T; RISK FACTORS; **Publication Type:** journal article; meta-analysis. PMID: 11590087

Fischer MA, Avorn J (2004). Economic implications of evidence-based prescribing for hypertension: can better care cost less? *JAMA.* 2004 Apr 21;291(15):1850-6. **MeSH Terms:** AGED; *ANTIHYPERTENSIVE AGENTS (subheadings: economics; therapeutic use); COST SAVINGS; *EVIDENCE-BASED MEDICINE (subheading: economics); FEMALE; HUMANS; *HYPERTENSION (subheadings: drug therapy; economics); MALE; PENNSYLVANIA; PRACTICE GUIDELINES RESEARCH SUPPORT, U.S. GOV'T, P.H.S.; **Publication Type:** journal article. PMID: 15100203

Flegal KM, Williamson DF, et al (2004). Estimating deaths attributable to obesity in the United States. *Am J Public Health.* 2004 Sep;94(9):1486-9. **MeSH Terms:** ADULT; AGE DISTRIBUTION; AGED; AGED, 80 AND OVER; BIAS (subheading: epidemiology); CAUSE OF DEATH; COHORT STUDIES; *DEATH CERTIFICATES; FEMALE; *HEALTH STATUS; HUMANS; MALE; MIDDLE AGED; *OBESITY (subheadings: mortality; prevention & control); *POPULATION SURVEILLANCE (subheading: methods); PREVALENCE; RISK; UNITED STATES (subheading: epidemiology); **Publication Type:** clinical trial; journal article; review; review, tutorial. PMID: 15333299

Fretheim A, Aaserud M, et al (2003). The potential savings of using thiazides as the first choice antihypertensive drug: cost-minimisation analysis. *BMC Health Serv Res.* 2003 Sep 08;3(1):18. **MeSH Terms:** ADULT; *ANTIHYPERTENSIVE AGENTS (subheadings: economics; therapeutic use); CANADA; COMPARATIVE STUDY; *COST SAVINGS (subheading: statistics & numerical data); DECISION MAKING; *DIURETICS, THIAZIDE (subheadings: economics; therapeutic use); *DRUG COSTS (subheading: statistics & numerical data); DRUG UTILIZATION (subheadings: economics; standards); EUROPE; HEALTH EXPENDITURES (subheading: statistics & numerical data); HUMANS; *HYPERTENSION (subheadings: drug therapy; economics); *PRACTICE GUIDELINES; PRESCRIPTIONS, DRUG (subheading: economics); SENSITIVITY AND SPECIFICITY; UNITED STATES; **Publication Type:** journal article. PMID: 12959644

Gerberding JL, Marks JS (2004). Making America fit and trim--steps big and small. *Am J Public Health.* 2004 Sep;94(9):1478-9. **MeSH**

Terms: ADOLESCENT; ADOLESCENT BEHAVIOR (subheading: psychology); CHILD; CHILD BEHAVIOR (subheading: psychology); HEALTH BEHAVIOR; *HEALTH EDUCATION (subheading: standards); *HEALTH PROMOTION (subheading: standards); HUMANS; *OBESITY (subheadings: epidemiology; prevention & control); PREVALENCE; RISK FACTORS; SCHOOL HEALTH SERVICES (subheading: standards); UNITED STATES (subheading: epidemiology); **Publication Type:** editorial; journal article; review; review, tutorial. PMID: 15333297

Hamajima N, Hirose K, et al (2002). Alcohol, tobacco and breast cancer--collaborative reanalysis of individual data from 53 epidemiological studies, including 58,515 women with breast cancer and 95,067 women without the disease. *Br J Cancer.* 2002 Nov 18;87(11):1234-45. **MeSH Terms:** ADULT; AGED; *ALCOHOL DRINKING (subheading: adverse effects); *BREAST NEOPLASMS (subheadings: epidemiology; etiology); CARDIOVASCULAR DISEASES (subheading: etiology); *DEVELOPING COUNTRIES; EPIDEMIOLOGIC STUDIES; FEMALE; HUMANS; INCIDENCE; MIDDLE AGED; RESEARCH SUPPORT, NON-U.S. GOV'T; RISK ASSESSMENT; *SMOKING (subheading: adverse effects); **Publication Type:** comment; journal article; meta-analysis. PMID: 12439712

Herman WW, Konzelman JL Jr, Prisant LM (2004). New national guidelines on hypertension: a summary for dentistry. *J Am Dent Assoc.* 2004 May;135(5):576-84. **MeSH Terms:** ANTIHYPERTENSIVE AGENTS (subheading: therapeutic use); BLOOD PRESSURE DETERMINATION; CONSENSUS; *DENTAL CARE FOR CHRONICALLY ILL; HUMANS; *HYPERTENSION (subheadings: classification; diagnosis; therapy); LIFE STYLE; TERMINOLOGY; **Publication Type:** guideline; journal article; practice guideline; review; review, tutorial. PMID: 15202748

Kaplan NM (2004). What can we expect from new guidelines? *Med Clin North Am.* 2004 Jan;88(1):141-8, ix. **MeSH Terms:** ADULT; AGED; *ANTIHYPERTENSIVE AGENTS (subheading: therapeutic use); HUMANS; *HYPERTENSION (subheadings: diet therapy; drug therapy; epidemiology); INCIDENCE; *LIFE STYLE; MIDDLE AGED; NUTRITION SURVEYS; *PHYSICIAN'S ROLE; *PRACTICE GUIDELINES; TREATMENT REFUSAL; UNITED STATES (subheading: epidemiology); **Publication Type:** journal article; review; review, tutorial. PMID: 14871056

Montori VM, Wilczynski NL, et al (2005). Optimal search strategies for retrieving systematic reviews from Medline: analytical survey. *BMJ.* 2005 Jan 8;330(7482):68. **MeSH Terms:** *INFORMATION STOR-

AGE AND RETRIEVAL (subheadings: methods; standards); *MEDLINE (subheading: standards); MEDICAL SUBJECT HEADINGS; RESEARCH SUPPORT, NON-U.S. GOV'T; RESEARCH SUPPORT, U.S. GOV'T, P.H.S.; *REVIEW LITERATURE; SENSITIVITY AND SPECIFICITY; **Publication Type:** journal article. PMID: 15619601

Nordmann AJ, Krahn M, et al (2003). The cost effectiveness of ACE inhibitors as first-line antihypertensive therapy. *Pharmacoeconomics.* 2003;21(8):573-85. **MeSH Terms:** ADRENERGIC BETA-ANTAGONISTS (subheadings: economics; therapeutic use); *ANGIOTENSIN-CONVERT-ING ENZYME INHIBITORS (subheadings: economics; therapeutic use); CANADA (subheading: epidemiology); COHORT STUDIES; COMPARA-TIVE STUDY; COST-BENEFIT ANALYSIS; DIURETICS (subheadings: economics; therapeutic use); DRUG UTILIZATION (subheadings: economics; statistics & numerical data); HUMANS; *HYPERTENSION (subheadings: complications; drug therapy); HYPERTROPHY, LEFT VENTRICULAR (subheadings: complications; drug therapy; economics); MARKOV CHAINS; PRACTICE GUIDELINES; QUALITY-ADJUSTED LIFE YEARS; RANDOMIZED CONTROLLED TRIALS; RESEARCH SUPPORT, NON-U.S. GOV'T; **Publication Type:** journal article. PMID: 12751915

Shojania KG, Bero LA (2001). Taking advantage of the explosion of systematic reviews: an efficient MEDLINE search strategy. *Eff Clin Pract.* 2001 Jul-Aug;4(4):157-62. **MeSH Terms:** *EVIDENCE-BASED MEDICINE; HUMANS; *INFORMATION STORAGE AND RETRIEVAL (subheading: methods); *MEDLINE; *META-ANALYSIS; *REVIEW LIT-ERATURE; SENSITIVITY AND SPECIFICITY; SUBJECT HEADINGS; USER-COMPUTER INTERFACE; **Publication Type:** evaluation studies; journal article. PMID: 11525102

Smith-Warner SA, Spiegelman D, et al (1998). Alcohol and breast cancer in women: a pooled analysis of cohort studies. *JAMA* 279(7): 535-40. **MeSH Terms:** ALCOHOL DRINKING; *BREAST NEOPLASMS (subheading: epidemiology); DIET; ESTROGEN REPLACEMENT THERAPY; FEMALE; HUMAN; LIKELIHOOD FUNCTIONS; LINEAR MODELS; MENARCHE; MENOPAUSE; MULTIVARIATE ANALYSIS; PROSPECTIVE STUDIES; RE-GRESSION ANALYSIS; RISK; STATISTICS, NONPARAMETRIC; SUPPORT, NON-U.S. GOV'T; SUPPORT, U.S. GOV'T, P.H.S.; **Publication Type:** journal article; meta-analysis. PMID: 9480365

Steinman MA, Fischer MA, et al (2004). Clinician awareness of adherence to hypertension guidelines. *Am J Med.* 2004 Nov 15;117(10):747-54.

MeSH Terms: AGED; *ANTIHYPERTENSIVE AGENTS (subheading: therapeutic use); CHI-SQUARE DISTRIBUTION; FEMALE; *GUIDELINE ADHERENCE; HUMANS; *HYPERTENSION (subheading: drug therapy); LOGISTIC MODELS; MALE; MIDDLE AGED; *PHYSICIAN'S PRACTICE PATTERNS (subheading: statistics & numerical data); *PRACTICE GUIDELINES; QUESTIONNAIRES; RESEARCH SUPPORT, U.S. GOV'T, NON-P.H.S.; UNITED STATES; VETERANS; **Publication Type:** journal article. PMID: 15541324

Willett WC and Stampfer MJ (1997). Sobering data on alcohol and breast cancer. *Epidemiology* 8(3): 225-7. **MeSH:** *ALCOHOL DRINKING (subheading: adverse effects); *BREAST NEOPLASMS (subheading: etiology); CAUSALITY; FEMALE; HUMAN; RISK FACTORS; **Publication Type:** comment; editorial. PMID: 9115012

Williams B, Poulter NR, et al (2004). British Hypertension Society guidelines for hypertension management 2004 (BHS-IV): summary. *BMJ*. 2004 Mar 13;328(7440):634-40. **MeSH Terms:** ALGORITHMS; ANTIHYPERTENSIVE AGENTS (subheading: therapeutic use); ASPIRIN (subheading: therapeutic use); BLOOD PRESSURE DETERMINATION (subheading: methods); CARDIOVASCULAR DISEASES (subheadings: etiology; prevention & control); HUMANS; HYDROXYMETHYLGLU-TARYL-COA REDUCTASE INHIBITORS (subheading: therapeutic use); *HYPERTENSION (subheadings: prevention & control; therapy); LIFE STYLE; MEDICAL HISTORY TAKING (subheading: methods); PHYSICAL EXAMINATION (subheading: methods); PLATELET AGGREGATION INHIBITORS (subheading: therapeutic use); RISK ASSESSMENT; **Publication Type:** guideline; journal article; practice guideline. PMID: 15016698

Zhang Y, Kreger BE, et al (1999). Alcohol consumption and risk of breast cancer: the Framingham Study revisited. *Am J Epidemiol* 149(2): 93-101. **MeSH Terms:** ADULT; AGED; *ALCOHOL DRINKING (subheading: adverse effects); ALCOHOLIC BEVERAGES (subheadings: adverse effects; classification); BODY MASS INDEX; *BREAST NEOPLASMS (subheadings: epidemiology; etiology); FEMALE; FOLLOW-UP STUDIES; HUMAN; IN-CIDENCE; MASSACHUSETTS (subheading: epidemiology); MENOPAUSE; MIDDLE AGE; MULTIVARIATE ANALYSIS; PREGNANCY; RISK FACTORS; SUPPORT, NON-U.S. GOV'T; SUPPORT, U.S. GOV'T, P.H.S.; **Publication Type:** journal article. PMID: 9921953

5

Framing Questions and
Other Practical Tips

W HEN you begin to use Medical Subject Headings and the other special indexing features that are built into MEDLINE, your searches will become more productive. Practice helps too. Meanwhile, here are some suggestions.

Getting Started

Before doing an extensive MEDLINE search, make sure you understand the topic you are searching. Review articles are helpful in this regard. Is there an electronic book, guideline, or other resource that might answer your question? Many questions do not require a MEDLINE search, which is inevitably more time-consuming than a quick lookup in a book or electronic resource (see "Health Information on the Web" in Appendix A). Even if inadequate, a resource that synthesizes or synopsizes can help to sharpen your thinking about what, precisely, is to be asked in a MEDLINE search.

Before connecting to MEDLINE, write out the key concepts that you wish to explore. What MeSH terms might best capture these concepts? If you are not sure, take advantage of on-line MeSH resources.

Be Specific

Be specific in framing your question. You don't want to find all the citations concerning HYPERTENSION or ASTHMA or ACQUIRED

IMMUNODEFICIENCY SYNDROME. Common medical problems such as these are the subject of more publications than you can possibly consider. For example, the MeSH term HYPERTENSION is attached to more than 800 new citations each month. What is it about HYPERTENSION that one might wish to know? Information about drug therapy in the elderly? (If so, HYPERTENSION with the subheading "drug therapy" attached to it AND AGED might be a good place to start.) Adherence to prescribed therapy for high blood pressure among blacks? (If so, PATIENT COMPLIANCE AND HYPERTENSION AND African Americans would probably be a useful strategy.)

Be Inquisitive

Even if your search seems to have been successful, ask yourself, "What trade-offs have I made in following this particular search strategy?" If you made careful use of Medical Subject Headings for a precisely targeted search, you might have missed something that would have been captured with a broader MeSH term, though such a reformulated search would be done at the expense of turning up many irrelevant papers. Conversely, you may have started with too broadly focused a search strategy and then employed narrowing strategies that threw out potentially useful citations. Did you make use of the Major Topic option to focus your search? Though powerful in focusing search results, relying too heavily on this option can cause you to miss useful citations. Would the use of a particular subheading or publication type have better focused the search? Or, did the use of subheadings and publication types filter out potentially useful papers? There is no perfect way to search. *Effective searching is an iterative process that involves both narrowing and widening strategies.*

The only way to answer these questions is to try a few reformulated searches. You might try some Text Word searches, displaying the Medical Subject Headings for the citations that appear to be most promising. Sometimes a combination of MeSH terms and Text Words is helpful. If you have found an article that looks useful, take advantage of PubMed's "Related Articles" link, which uses a powerful algorithm based on Medical Subject Headings and Text Words.

Experiment with various approaches. Whenever you find useful citations, examine how they were indexed.

Ask the Right Question

Perceiving the question that best illuminates a practical problem requires skills that are completely unrelated to MEDLINE but have everything to do with its effective application. Several years ago, the residents of the most highly industrialized neighborhood in San Francisco were concerned about the health risks that might be associated with a thermoelectric power plant that was planned for construction within their community. There was a higher-than-expected rate of breast cancer within the community, so opposition to the construction of the power plant was initially framed in terms of this specific health risk. Does industrial pollution, specifically that associated with power plants, increase the risk of breast cancer? This is a reasonable question, but its answer—that the link between environmental pollution and breast cancer did not seem strong enough to challenge the construction of the power plant—was entirely unsatisfactory to community members. The preventable risks for breast cancer might have been explored, but the community was alarmed by the prospect of health risks that might be attributed to environmental pollution from the proposed power plant. Stepping back and reassessing the situation, it was apparent that ASTHMA was (and remains) a major health problem in that community. Re-framing the question in terms of the role of ENVIRONMENTAL POLLUTION, particularly AIR POLLUTION, in causing ASTHMA was more fruitful in supporting the community's concern about the proposed power plant construction. There is even a specific literature about POWER PLANTS AND ASTHMA (Levy, Greco et al 2002; Henry, Abramson et al 1991; Halliday, Henry et al 1993; Goren and Hellmann 1997).

Evaluating Results

The breadth and depth of information covered in MEDLINE make it inevitable that some of what you find will be off the mark. Some citations will identify themselves as superfluous to your purpose by their titles. Others might appear to be what you are looking for, until you read their abstracts or examine their indexing. The journal that published the paper, the type of publication, and controversy about what is known are three things to keep in mind as you review your search results:

Journals. Journals, like the audiences for which they are intended, vary widely. The same topic will be treated quite differently in a journal that primarily publishes reviews for practicing clinicians, compared with a journal that publishes both research and reviews, or a journal that is primarily intended for non-clinical researchers. In addition, there are journals aimed at every type of practicing clinician, and there are many kinds of research. Journal editors pay careful attention to the framing of questions addressed by authors, publishing only those papers that reflect the mission of the journal and the corresponding interests of the journal's audience. You can use this intellectual filter as a limiting strategy, by searching in a subset of journals, or by simply noting the journals in which promising-looking titles were published.

Publication Type and MeSH Term. Even publications within the same journal might address related issues in different ways—as letters, clinical trials, reviews, or other types of publication. For example, in 1998 the *New England Journal of Medicine* published two quite different papers that were both indexed under ESTROGEN REPLACEMENT THERAPY AND OSTEOPOROSIS, POSTMENOPAUSAL. One of them was a review entitled the "Treatment of Postmenopausal Osteoporosis" (Eastell 1998), and the other was a randomized controlled trial entitled "Prevention of Bone Loss with Alendronate in Postmenopausal Women under 60 Years of Age" (Hosking, Chilvers et al 1998). As you can see from looking at the other aspects of the indexing of these two papers (see References), they are indexed quite differently in MEDLINE. Information of this sort can be useful for refocusing subsequent searches.

Conflicting Information. You will sometimes find conflicting information. Like the proverbial blind men who inspected the trunk, leg, side, and tail of the same elephant and were unable to agree as to the elephant's shape, different researchers sometimes come up with different slices of the same reality. MEDLINE is full of rigorous study and spirited debate about the answers to seemingly basic questions. Controversial issues are sometimes the topic of review papers. A practice guideline or meta-analysis, if available, can be quite helpful. Editorials and letters to the editor often provide commentary that will help you understand the context in which a paper might be understood. Citations to editorials and letters to the editor are included in the "Comment in" field of the MEDLINE record for articles; they will probably turn up in your search results as well. Take your time; collect all of the available evidence and weigh it.

Read Beyond Abstracts

MEDLINE's on-line abstracts provide an excellent means for superficially digesting a wide range of literature, but an abstract can be seductive. It gives one the sense of knowing what is contained in a paper without having expended the effort and time necessary to obtain and read it. In some instances, abstracts provide sufficient information for the question at hand, but abstracts must be recognized for what they are. Abstracts are written by authors; at worst, they can present a biased account of the evidence that they describe. Structured abstracts, required by some journals, present a paper's contents in a uniform manner, summarizing the study's background, methods, results, and conclusions. Nevertheless, even the best abstract necessarily omits most of the information upon which it is based. The authors will qualify and appraise their results in a discussion section that cannot be captured in an abstract. Critical reading of a paper will sharpen your thinking about the issues and evidence that are described in it. In some cases, you may question the authors' methods, or the way that they interpreted the evidence upon which they drew their conclusions. No one would argue with the assertion that *papers need to be read in their entirety to be fully appreciated,* but the power of MEDLINE to bring so much evidence so quickly to our computer screens makes it important to state the obvious.

The number of journals in PubMed Central (PMC)—the National Library of Medicine's digital archive of life sciences journal literature—is growing rapidly. Access to the full text of articles in PMC is free.

Photocopies of papers can be ordered on-line at a modest cost. Many journals now publish on-line full-text versions. These may require a subscription fee to help subsidize the journal's work, though an increasing number of journals are allowing free access to their older issues (usually older than one year). Most medical libraries have on-line journal subscriptions; authorized users are able to access these remotely.

Although MEDLINE searches will cause you to read more widely than you might otherwise, continued subscriptions to your favorite journals remain a valuable means for keeping current. Searches that are limited to the journals in your personal collection can make the contents of that collection more accessible to you, even though the journals themselves may be on shelves that are only feet away from your computer. And the on-line full-text access that accompanies many journal subscriptions can be a great convenience when your personal collection of journals is not handy (or is not well organized enough for rapid access). The *New England Journal of Medicine, JAMA, Annals of Internal Medicine, American Journal of Public Health, Pediatrics, American Journal of Health-System Pharmacy* and the *American Heart Journal* are a few of the journals that provide such on-line access to regular subscribers. The National Library of

Medicine maintains links to a growing number of journal publisher Web sites (see Appendix A).

Are You Looking in the Right Place?

Your searches will lead you first to the most recent few years of publications. This will give you a snapshot of the latest in what may be a prolonged inquiry into the subject you are pursuing. The question you are trying to answer may have been addressed insightfully a decade ago. Don't ignore older papers. Using the search-focusing tools described in this book, you can scan decades of literature very quickly.

The National Library of Medicine produces a number of other databases that may be helpful in answering your question. The NLM Catalog provides bibliographic information on books, journals, and other materials via the Entrez retrieval system. If you are familiar with PubMed, you will feel at home with the NLM Catalog. As in PubMed, entry terms for NLM Catalog searches are mapped to MeSH terms, and you can also use MeSH terms in your query for better results.

Another Entrez resource is Bookshelf, a growing collection of online biomedical books. You can search Bookshelf directly, or you can follow the Links>Books link on the right-hand side of any PubMed citation to see a special display that includes links from many of its words to pages in books where the word appears.

The Entrez search page allows you to search across all of its databases, and it provides links to each of its databases, allowing you to search the one that seems most appropriate.

These and other NLM resources are described more fully in Appendix A.

The Web in its entirety contains a great deal of useful health information, along with a much larger amount of information that you will not want to see. Some helpful links are provided in Appendix A.

Keep Track of What You Have Learned

Use your reprint files to remind yourself of Medical Subject Headings and strategies that have been useful in previous searches. Simply writing these on the front of a reprint can be quite helpful at a later date. If you are printing the full-text version of an article, you can also print out a MEDLINE display that includes its MeSH indexing information (the Citation display in PubMed does this neatly), and staple it to the article. Or, if you are headed to the library to photocopy some papers, you can use this as a means for locating your articles, appending it to the article's pages as you staple them. If you use bibliographic management software such as EndNote® and download your citations from MEDLINE into this software, the resulting libraries on your computer's hard drive will contain Medical Subject Heading information that can be studied for subsequent searches. Make use of PMIDs to return to citations, to see how they were indexed.

Search results and search strategies can be saved in Entrez's "My NCBI." If you are creating Web pages, the URLs for search strategies can be included as links.

Conclusion

MEDLINE's controlled vocabulary and elaborate indexing system require a little effort, but the reward for understanding this powerful tool is more direct access to the accumulated knowledge that resides in the medical literature. Take advantage of all the energy that has gone into organizing the information in MEDLINE. It is a National treasure.

References

Eastell R (1998). "Treatment of postmenopausal osteoporosis." *N Engl J Med* 338(11): 736-46. **MeSH Terms:** CALCITONIN (subheading: therapeutic use); CALCIUM (subheading: therapeutic use); DIPHOSPHO-

NATES (subheading: therapeutic use); DRUG EVALUATION; ESTROGEN REPLACEMENT THERAPY; FEMALE; FLUORIDES (subheading: therapeutic use); HUMAN; *OSTEOPOROSIS, POSTMENOPAUSAL (subheadings: diagnosis; drug therapy; physiopathology); RISK FACTORS; VITAMIN D (subheading: therapeutic use); **Publication Type:** journal article; review; review, tutorial. PMID: 9494151

Goren, A. I. and S. Hellmann (1997). "Has the prevalence of asthma increased in children? Evidence from a long term study in Israel." *J Epidemiol Community Health* 51(3): 227-32. **MeSH Terms:** AIR POLLUTION (subheading: analysis); *ASTHMA (subheadings: epidemiology; physiopathology); BRONCHITIS (subheading: epidemiology); CHILD; COHORT STUDIES; COUGH (subheading: epidemiology); FEMALE; FOLLOW-UP STUDIES; FORCED EXPIRATORY VOLUME (subheading: physiology); HUMAN; ISRAEL (subheading: epidemiology); LOGISTIC MODELS; MALE; ODDS RATIO; POWER PLANTS; PREVALENCE; RESPIRATORY SOUNDS (subheading: physiopathology); RISK FACTORS; SUPPORT, NON-U.S. GOV'T; VITAL CAPACITY (subheading: physiology); **Publication Type:** journal article. PMID: 9229049

Halliday, J. A., R. L. Henry, et al. (1993). "Increased wheeze but not bronchial hyperreactivity near power stations." *J Epidemiol Community Health* 47(4): 282-6. **MeSH Terms:** *ASTHMA (subheadings: epidemiology; etiology); *BRONCHIAL HYPERREACTIVITY (subheadings: epidemiology; etiology); CHILD; CHILD, PRESCHOOL; CROSS-SECTIONAL STUDIES; *ENVIRONMENTAL POLLUTION (subheading: adverse effects); FEMALE; HUMAN; MALE; NEW SOUTH WALES (subheading: epidemiology); POWER PLANTS; PREVALENCE; *RESPIRATORY SOUNDS (subheading: etiology); SUPPORT, NON-U.S. GOV'T; **Publication Type:** journal article. PMID: 8228762

Henry, R. L., R. Abramson, et al. (1991). "Asthma in the vicinity of power stations: I. A prevalence study." *Pediatr Pulmonol* 11(2): 127-33. **MeSH Terms:** *AIR POLLUTION (subheading: adverse effects); *ASTHMA (subheadings: epidemiology; etiology); CHILD; CROSS-SECTIONAL STUDIES; FEMALE; HUMAN; INCIDENCE; MALE; NEW SOUTH WALES (subheading: epidemiology); POWER PLANTS; RESPIRATORY HYPERSENSITIVITY (subheadings: epidemiology; etiology); RESPIRATORY TRACT INFECTIONS (subheadings: epidemiology; etiology); RISK FACTORS; SUPPORT, NON-U.S. GOV'T; **Publication Type:** journal article. PMID: 1758730

Hosking, D., C. E. Chilvers, et al. (1998). "Prevention of bone loss with alendronate in postmenopausal women under 60 years of age. Early Postmenopausal Intervention Cohort Study Group." *N Engl J Med* 338(8): 485-92. **MeSH Terms:** *ALENDRONATE (subheadings: adverse effects; pharmacology; therapeutic use); *BONE DENSITY (subheading: drug effects); COMPARATIVE STUDY; DOUBLE-BLIND METHOD; DRUG COMBINATIONS; ESTROGEN REPLACEMENT THERAPY; *ESTROGENS, CONJUGATED (subheadings: pharmacology; therapeutic use); FEMALE; FOREARM; HUMAN; LUMBAR VERTEBRAE (subheading: drug effects); *MEDROXYPROGESTERONE (subheadings: pharmacology; therapeutic use); MIDDLE AGE; *OSTEOPOROSIS, POSTMENOPAUSAL (subheading: prevention & control); PELVIC BONES (subheading: drug effects); POSTMENOPAUSE; PROGESTATIONAL HORMONES, SYNTHETIC (subheadings pharmacology; therapeutic use); SUPPORT, NON-U.S. GOV'T; **Publication Type:** clinical trial; journal article; multicenter study; randomized controlled trial. PMID: 9443925

Levy JI, Greco SL, et al (2002). The importance of population susceptibility for air pollution risk assessment: a case study of power plants near Washington, DC. *Environ Health Perspect.* 2002 Dec;110(12):1253-60. **MeSH Terms:** ADOLESCENT; ADULT; AFRICAN CONTINENTAL ANCESTRY GROUP; AGED; *AIR POLLUTANTS, ENVIRONMENTAL (subheadings: adverse effects; economics); *AIR POLLUTION (subheadings: economics; prevention & control); ASTHMA (subheadings: etiology; prevention & control; therapy); CARDIOVASCULAR DISEASES (subheadings: etiology; prevention & control; therapy); CHILD; CHILD, PRESCHOOL; DIABETES COMPLICATIONS; DISTRICT OF COLUMBIA (subheading: epidemiology); EDUCATIONAL STATUS; EPIDEMIOLOGIC STUDIES; FEMALE; GEOGRAPHY; HUMANS; INFANT; INFANT, NEWBORN; LIFE EXPECTANCY; MALE; MIDDLE AGED; MINORITY GROUPS; *MODELS, THEORETICAL; *MORTALITY (subheading: trends); PATIENT ADMISSION (subheading: statistics & numerical data); POVERTY; *POWER PLANTS; *PUBLIC HEALTH; RESEARCH SUPPORT, NON-U.S. GOV'T; RESEARCH SUPPORT, U.S. GOV'T, P.H.S.; **Publication Type:** journal article. PMID: 12460806

Appendix A

MEDLINE Interfaces and Related Resources on the World Wide Web

A Web-based version* of this appendix,
with active links, is available at:
www.ashburypress.com/medline/resources

THIS appendix will help you to locate a source for MEDLINE, if you don't already have one. It also describes useful MEDLINE-related resources, including other sources of health information. Some of these are within the National Library of Medicine's Web site (**www.nlm.nih.gov**), which is among the most important health sites on the Web.

MEDLINE from the National Library of Medicine (NLM)

The National Library of Medicine, which produces MEDLINE and licenses it to other vendors, provides free access on its Web site:

PubMed

If you are not already using MEDLINE, PubMed (**www.pubmed.gov**) is the best place to start (unless you are starting out at an academic institution that uses Ovid). PubMed is very fast, easy to use, and has excellent on-line MeSH help. PubMed provides context-specific links to other Entrez databases (**www.ncbi.nlm.nih.gov/gquery/gquery.fcgi?itool=toolbar**) and

---

*This printed version corresponds to the January 15, 2006 update of the Web page. Suggestions are welcome: E-mail: **brian.katcher@gmail.com**

to resources beyond the National Library of Medicine. Among experienced searchers not using a particular university-based MEDLINE interface, this has become the de facto standard. The search examples in this book are based on searches with this implementation of MEDLINE.

PubMed is MEDLINE with additional citations that have not yet been indexed for MEDLINE or are beyond its scope, as well as citations from OLDMEDLINE (pre-1966 citations). An NLM Fact Sheet explains the difference between MEDLINE and PubMed (**www.nlm.nih.gov/pubs/ factsheets/dif_med_pub.html**).

For serious searches in any MEDLINE interface, you will want to give some thought to the MeSH that best describe the concepts you are researching, and PubMed's MeSH Database (**www.ncbi.nlm.nih.gov/ entrez/query.fcgi?db=mesh**) is particularly helpful in this regard. In fact, you can even construct your search strategy from within this well-designed MeSH Database, which can be reached from a link on the left side of the PubMed home page. PubMed's Citation Display contains links from the MeSH terms assigned to each article; these can be used to find more information, or they can be used as the basis for a new search strategy.

The limits options in PubMed allow you to restrict your searches by Publication Type (such as Clinical Trial, Meta-Analysis, Practice Guideline, Review, or Randomized Controlled Trial), language, subsets (such as Abridged Index Medicus, Complementary Medicine, Nursing, Dental, or AIDS), and other elements that are built into MEDLINE.

PubMed's Clinical Queries and Special Queries filters provide a handy means for starting a search. After an initial search, you will probably want to construct additional search strategies based on what you have learned.

After you have done a search, use the "Details" tab to see how PubMed has processed your search. For more information about each element, see PubMed Help (**www.ncbi.nlm.nih.gov/books/bv.fcgi?rid=helppubmed. chapter.pubmedhelp**) or NLM's more detailed MEDLINE/PubMed Data Element Descriptions (**www.nlm.nih.gov/bsd/mms/medlineelements. html**) information page.

To get the most out of this interface, take a look at PubMed's Tutorial (linked from the PubMed home page).

Gateway

Gateway (**http://gateway.nlm.nih.gov/gw/Cmd**) is intended for users who come to the National Library of Medicine without knowing what is there or how best to search for it. NLM Gateway provides a single interface for searching in a number of the Library's resources, including PubMed, MedlinePlus (described below, under "Health Information on the Web"), the NLM Catalog, ClinicalTrials.gov, DIRLINE (Directory of Health Organizations), and others. NLM Gateway's most remarkable feature is that it searches simultaneously within multiple retrieval systems. Its Find Terms button leads you to information about the Medical Subject Headings (MeSH) that might encompass the terms you enter.

If you know that what you are looking for is in MEDLINE, then PubMed is a more appropriate interface, because its limits feature is specific to MEDLINE. (The limits button in the NLM Gateway is for categories, such as journal articles, consumer health, books/serials/AV, or databanks.) However, NLM Gateway provides access to much more information than can be found in MEDLINE. A full description of what's available from NLM Gateway can be found on its "About" page.

Other Sources of MEDLINE on the Web

PubMed (public site) and Ovid (many institutions) are the most widely used, but there are other interfaces to MEDLINE on the Web. Some are free, some are free with registration, and some are fee-based. A sampling: Medscape (**http://intapp.medscape.com/px/medlineapp/ medline?cid=med&adv=1**) (a Web site for clinicians), Infotrieve (**http:// www4.infotrieve.com/newmedline/search.asp**) (specializes in document delivery), and PaperChase (**www.paperchase.com**).

If you are affiliated with a major teaching institution, you can probably apply for a remote access account that will make your home or office computer screen look like the one in the library. Such libraries generally use either the Ovid interface to MEDLINE or a customized version of PubMed that has been tailored to best serve the library's patrons. In addition, many university libraries offer full-text access to a growing number of on-line journals for which they have paid subscriptions. (See Journals on the Web.) For copyright reasons, remote access is limited to those with library privileges.

Medical Subject Headings (MeSH)

The usefulness of Medical Subject Headings (MeSH) is an underlying theme of this book.

An excellent publicly available resource for using MeSH is the Entrez

MeSH Database (www.ncbi.nlm.nih.gov/entrez/query.fcgi?db=mesh). A link can be found on the PubMed search screen. The MeSH Database home page includes links to three excellent tutorials.

Use the MeSH Database to determine what concepts from this controlled vocabulary best describe your search topic. PubMed search strategies can be constructed from within this database.

When you find an interesting article in PubMed, use the Citation display to see the MeSH terms that were used to index it. Each of these MeSH terms (some of them with subheadings, some of them as Major MeSH) will appear as a hyperlink. You can use these links to learn more about these MeSH. You can also use them as the basis for a new search (selected MeSH terms will be searched exactly as they were applied to the citation—with subheadings, etc). You may see additional Entrez database search links options for some terms. If there are substances in the display, they may include links to PubChem databases (http://pubchem.ncbi.nlm.nih.gov/).

Other MeSH resources from the National Library of Medicine include what might be called a "Medical Subject Headings Home Page," (www.nlm.nih.gov/mesh/meshhome.html) with links to a number of other MeSH-related resources, including a Fact Sheet with detailed information about MeSH and a MeSH Browser. (For most users, the MeSH Database will be more useful.)

The National Library of Medicine's Unified Medical Language System (UMLS) (www.nlm.nih.gov/research/umls) links other controlled vocabularies to MeSH. Among these are RxNorm (standard names for clinical drugs) (www.nlm.nih.gov/research/umls/rxnorm), SNOMED CT (the College of American Pathologists' Systematized Nomenclature of Medicine–Clinical Terms) (www.nlm.nih.gov/research/umls/Snomed/snomed_main.html), and more than 100 other source vocabularies. PubMed and the Entrez MeSH Database use the Unified Medical Language System to link entry terms to MeSH.

MEDLINE Tutorials

The National Library of Medicine's PubMed Tutorial (www.nlm.nih.gov/bsd/disted/pubmed.html) will provide you with an excellent overview of PubMed and the MeSH vocabulary. It also provides help in using MyNCBI. Whether you normally use this or another source of MEDLINE, the MeSH Vocabulary portion is worth reviewing. The three MeSH tutorials can also be accessed from PubMed's MeSH Database (**www.ncbi.nlm.nih.gov/entrez/query.fcgi?db=mesh**).

Many institutional libraries use Ovid MEDLINE and have created their own Web-based tutorials (also of value for users of PubMed and other interfaces to MEDLINE). Try a Google (**www.google.com**) search for MEDLINE tutorials.

If your institutional library offers MEDLINE classes, take one.

In-Process Citations in PubMed

It takes some time for articles to be indexed for MEDLINE. High-profile journals like *JAMA* or the *New England Journal of Medicine* are indexed within days, but other journals take weeks to months. As citations are received from publishers, before they are indexed for MEDLINE, they are placed in PubMed (**www.pubmed.gov**) and are available from the default query box. These citations are based on the electronic files received from the publisher and are marked with one of two tags: "PubMed – as supplied by publisher" (as they are added) or, more commonly, "PubMed – in process" (accuracy of bibliographic data being reviewed and MeSH vocabulary being assigned, if the article is within the scope of MEDLINE).

If you search by author, journal, or unqualified words, these in-process citations will appear at the top of your search results. Further down you will see citations whose Medical Subject Headings (MeSH), Publication Types, Substance Names, and other indexing elements have been added. These are tagged as "PubMed – indexed for MEDLINE."

While it is generally preferable to use all of the indexing features that are built into MEDLINE, you may wish to augment your searches with in-process citations.

There are several ways to keep track of in-process citations. If you are interested in a particular journal, you can see its articles as they are added to PubMed. Just enter the full name or its official abbreviation (for help see the Journals Database—**www.ncbi.nlm.nih.gov/entrez/query.fcgi?db=journals**—which can be reached from PubMed). If you subscribe to a journal, you may be able to have the table of contents e-mailed to you upon publication. Most journals publish the table of contents of the most recent issue on their Web site (see Journals on the Web, on the next page). You can also store a pre-constructed search strategy in "My NCBI" (a PubMed service) and have the results sent to you by e-mail.

Journals on the Web

Many journals are available on the Web in full text, but free access is often limited to subscribers. Most academic medical center libraries maintain online subscriptions for students and faculty (Links to full-text journal articles can be found within Ovid or PubMed searches, depending on the institution).

When you see the orange green banner icon in the Summary display of your PubMed search results, it means you can see the full text article for free. An increasing number of journals provide free full text access to all or some of their articles, sometimes within six months or a year after initial publication. Here are some additional sources of free full text articles:

PubMed Central

The National Library of Medicine's PubMed Central (**www.ncbi.nlm. nih.gov:80/entrez/query.fcgi?db=PMC&itool=toolbar**—linked from PubMed) is an archive of free full-text articles. Articles in PubMed Central are sometimes also available from the publishers' Web sites, but those in PubMed Central are published in a standard format to insure their permanence on the Web.

When you see the orange and green banner icon in the Summary display of your PubMed results, it means that the article can be found in PubMed Central. If you like, you can use the "limits" tab in PubMed and, under "subsets," limit your searches to PubMed Central.

Open Access Journals

An increasing number of journals are developing publishing models that facilitate free access to full text articles. Some institutions, such as the University of California at San Francisco, encourage researchers to consider publishing their work in open access or reasonably priced journals (**www. library.ucsf.edu/research/scholcomm/whatyoucando.html**) as a means of protecting scholarly communication. Here are some resources:

❖ Directory of Open Access Journals (DOAJ) (**www.doaj.org**)

❖ BioMed Central (**www.biomedcentral.com**)

❖ Public Library of Science (PLoS) (**www.plos.org**)

Finding Journal Names

If you need help in finding the name of a journal, try the Entrez Journals Database (**www.ncbi.nlm.nih.gov/entrez/query.fcgi?db=journals**). The opening page also provides the means to find information about Entrez journals that have links to full-text web sites.

Articles Not Available on the Web

Much of what you find in MEDLINE, will not be available on the Web as a full-text document, but you can still obtain a copy if you do not have convenient access to a medical library. The National Library of Medicine's Loansome Doc allows you to order documents after first establishing an agreement with a nearby medical library. Detailed information about Loansome Doc (**www.nlm.nih.gov/pubs/factsheets/loansome_doc.html**) is available on the National Library of Medicine's Web Site, in the Fact Sheets section. Links to Loansome Doc are built into PubMed and NLM Gateway. Documents are available in a variety of forms (mail, fax, pickup, or internet), depending on the capacity of the local library. Charges vary, also depending on the local library.

If you have an My NCBI account (a free PubMed service), you can configure it for other document delivery services (Loansome Doc is the default).

NLM Resources

The National Library of Medicine (**www.nlm.nih.gov**) offers a wide array of Web-based resources in addition to MEDLINE, as can be seen from their home page and from their list of NLM Databases & Electronic Resources (**www.nlm.nih.gov/databases**). At this writing, there are 70 such resources—everything from accurate and clearly written health information for consumers (MedlinePlus) (**http://medlineplus.gov**) to the NLM Catalog (books, audiovisuals, journals, and electronic resources, all indexed with MeSH) (**www.ncbi.nlm.nih.gov/entrez/query.fcgi?db=nlmcatalog**) to the Visible Human Project (**www.nlm.nih.gov/research/visible/visible_human.html**) to a collection of online books (Bookshelf) (**www.ncbi.nlm.nih.gov/entrez/query.fcgi?db=Books**) to the National Center for Biotechnology Information (NCBI)'s Entrez databases (**www.ncbi.nlm.nih.gov/gquery/gquery.fcgi**) to the original *Index Catalogue of the Library of the Surgeon General's Office* that is described on pages 3–4 (**www.nlm.nih.gov/hmd/indexcat/ichome.html**).

You can save your PubMed search strategies by creating a free "My NCBI" account (a PubMed service). You can even schedule regular repeat searches and receive the results via e-mail.

The NLM Technical Bulletin (**www.nlm.nih.gov/pubs/techbull/**

tb.html) publishes information about changes as they occur, and back issues are well indexed.

Health Information on the Web

There is a tremendous amount of health information on the Web, but most of it suffers from two basic problems:

1. It varies widely in quality. When you find a new site, look to see who sponsors it, and determine its intended audience. Is it current? What is its evidence base? The Medical Library Association has a similar list of questions (**www.mlahq.org/resources/ medspeak/meddiag.html#topten**) on its site. MedlinePlus has a useful page of links, entitled Evaluating Health Information (**www.nlm.nih.gov/medlineplus/evaluatinghealthinformation. html**).

2. Unlike MEDLINE and other structured databases, most of the Web is completely unorganized. Search engines look at all the words on a Web page, as well as the links to and from the Web page (and, in some cases, additional criteria) for determining its ranking in response to a query. The ranking of "hits" from a search may or may not be suitable to your needs. Sometimes it's helpful to start elsewhere than Google.

Here is a sampling of useful places to go:

Interesting Search Tools

Google Scholar. In addition to its well-known main search page, Google offers a variety of specialized search pages. Google Scholar (**http://scholar. google.com**) uses Google's search algorithm, but its results are limited to articles and books of scholarly interest. According to Google, you can use it "to find articles from a wide variety of academic publishers, professional societies, preprint repositories and universities, as well as scholarly articles available across the Web." You can set Scholar's Preferences to show links within your affiliated medical library.

Searches for health information in Scholar will often point to PubMed (**www.pubmed.gov**) abstracts. When you find useful articles in Scholar, determine how they were indexed for PubMed (MeSH terms), and do another search in PubMed using these terms. Why? Because of the way that Scholar ranks hits, it is likely to miss the latest papers, and—more importantly—it lacks PubMed's ability to conduct Boolean searches based on the concepts that are represented by MeSH terms. You can see the MeSH terms for an article by displaying it in the "citation" format.

Google Scholar, still in beta at this writing, is attracting a lot of attention from medical librarians.

Scirus. Scirus (www.scirus.com/srsapp) limits its results to scientific information. Its default mode searches both journals and the Web, and its results page provides a link to each search. Less well known than Google Scholar, this is a powerful tool. Highly recommended.

OAIster (find the pearls...). OAIster (http://oaister.umdl.umich. edu/o/oaister) is the University of Michigan Digital Library's attempt at creating a collection of freely available, previously difficult-to-access, academically-oriented digital resources.

Practice Guidelines

Of course you can search for specific practice guidelines within MEDLINE by limiting your search to Publication Type "Practice Guideline" and following the links, but there are other resources for practice guidelines:

The National Guideline Clearinghouse (www.guideline.gov) is the Agency for Healthcare Research and Quality's (AHRQ) public archive for evidence-based clinical practice guidelines. AHRQ guidelines can also be accessed from HSTAT (Health Services/Technology Assessment Text) (www.ncbi.nlm.nih.gov/books/bv.fcgi?rid=hstat), which is an electronic book on the National Center for Biotechnology Information's Bookshelf (www.ncbi.nlm.nih.gov/entrez/query.fcgi?db=Books). These are all free full text resources.

Evidence Based Medicine

Some evidence based medicine resources require a subscription, but here is a sampling of free resources:

❖ Database of Abstracts of Reviews of Effectiveness (DARE) (www.york.ac.uk/inst/crd/darehp.htm)

❖ Cochrane Reviews Abstracts (www.cochrane.org/reviews)

❖ Systematic Reviews in PubMed (www.ncbi.nlm.nih.gov/entrez/ query/static/clinical.shtml#reviews). PubMed's Search by Clinical Study Category filter, on the same Web page, is also quite useful.

Consumer Sites

These sites are also useful for health professionals. The Medical Library Association (MLA) has produced a User's Guide to Finding and Evaluating Health Information on the Web (**www.mlanet.org/resources/ userguide.html**), which includes a list of their "top ten" most useful consumer Web sites. My own favorite is MedlinePlus (**www.medlineplus. gov**), which has links to carefully vetted health topic pages, a serviceable medical dictionary, links to patient drug information sheets, and links to all the current health news, in reverse chronological order (organized by day). Health-related stories are a staple of the media, and we often are questioned about them. This is a good way to find enough information to locate the study itself.

Libraries

Librarians are experts in the organization of intellectual resources (historically, this has been books), so it is not surprising that medical librarians have made significant attempts at organizing medical information on the Web. Here is a sampling:

- ❖ HealthWeb (**http://healthweb.org**), a collaborative project of health science libraries in the Greater Midwest Region of the US and the National Library of Medicine.

- ❖ The Recommended Core Collection of Web Sites for Hospital Libraries (**http://www4.umdnj.edu/camlbweb/CoreCollection. htm**), created by the Camden Campus Library of the University of Medicine & Dentistry of New Jersey, is another useful list of links.

- ❖ Hardin MD (**www.lib.uiowa.edu/hardin/md**) is a directory of directories, organized by topic areas. Links to more links. Compiled by Eric Rumsey at the Hardin Library for the Health Sciences at the University of Iowa—a very rich site.

- ❖ The National Library of Medicine (NLM) (**www.nlm.nih. gov**)—see NLM Resources.

- ❖ There are many such directories, but a different approach to using the Web is Jan's Search Tips (**http://janstips.blogspot. com**), which takes the form of a well-written blog. Quite a few MEDLINE-related tips can be found in its archives.

Academic medical center libraries subscribe to a variety of Web-based resources that can be accessed from the library (or remotely by affiliates of the library). A sampling:

- ❖ EMBASE—a bibliographic database with a somewhat different scope than MEDLINE. Offers extensive coverage of the drug and biomedical literature.

❖ Web of Science—A bibliographic database with excellent search capabilities for cited reference searching.

❖ Cochrane Database of Systematic Reviews—Evidence-based reviews of the clinical literature. Abstracts of the Cochrane Reviews are free-of-charge (**www.cochrane.org/reviews**).

❖ Drug Information Fulltext—Full text access to American Hospital Formulary Service Drug Information.

❖ Harrison's Online—Full text access to Harrison's Principles of Internal Medicine.

Librarians themselves are the best resource; visit your library.

U.S. Government

The National Institutes of Health (NIH) (**www.nih.gov**) is the premier institution for biomedical research. As you might expect, its Web site is huge. Each of its many institutes and centers (**www.nih.gov/icd**) has its own Web site. (The National Library of Medicine (NLM), which produces MEDLINE/PubMed, is part of NIH.)

The Department of Health and Human Services (**www.os.dhhs.gov**) is the overall government agency for health. Its Web site is designed for the general public. However, it also contains links to the various NIH institutes and centers, the Food and Drug Administration (FDA) (**www.fda.gov**), the Centers for Disease Control and Prevention (CDC) (**www.cdc.gov**), the Agency for Healthcare Research and Quality (AHRQ) (**www.ahrq. gov**), and other U.S. Government health agency Web sites.

The U.S. Government's role in biomedical research, public health, and health care delivery has been the subject of a great deal of literature, and it is all well indexed in MEDLINE. There are MeSH for each of the above-named agencies. To use these in your MEDLINE searches, go to the Enrez MeSH Database (**www.ncbi.nlm.nih.gov/entrez/query.fcgi?db=mesh**) and take a look. You can start by finding UNITED STATES DEPT. OF HEALTH AND HUMAN SERVICES and viewing its branches.

Public Health Sites

If you are working in public health, take advantage of Partners in Information Access for the Public Health Workforce (**http://phpartners.org**).

Other useful public health sites:

❖ Centers for Disease Control and Prevention (CDC) (**www.cdc. gov**)—The CDC, which is part of the U.S. Department of Health and Human Services, is arguably the largest public health agency on the planet. (It has twice as many staff as the World Health Organization.) As you might expect, the CDC site is huge; it's really many Web sites. You might try using Google to search it.

❖ World Health Organization (WHO) (**www.who.int/en/**)

❖ The Guide to Community Preventive Services (**www.thecommunityguide.org**) provides CDC-funded evidence-based reviews of interventions for common public health problems.

❖ Healthy People 2010 (**www.healthypeople.gov**)—National health promotion and disease prevention goals and objectives for us to attain by the year 2010! The entire document is on-line & can be viewed in portions…follow the "Publications" link to see links to the full text portions of the document. The HP2010 Information Access Project (**http://phpartners.org/hp**) provides links to the literature within specific HP2010 topic areas.

❖ Surgeon General Reports (**www.surgeongeneral.gov/library/reports.htm**)—Authoritative reports on important public health issues.

Professional Associations

A great deal of highly specialized health-related information on the Web is managed by specific professional associations. Become a member of the organizations that represent what you do.

Images

Google's wonderfully spare search page provides a link to Google Image Search (**www.google.com/imghp?hl=en&tab=wi&q=**), where you can find images to spruce up your presentations. Less well known but more powerful for serious educational purposes is HEAL (Health Education Assets Library) (**www.healcentral.org**). HEAL describes itself as "a digital library that provides freely accessible digital teaching resources of the highest quality that meet the needs of today's health sciences educators and learners." HEAL is peer reviewed, and its images are organized by MeSH. The CDC maintains a Public Health Image Library (**http://phil.cdc.gov/Phil/home.asp**). The National Library of Medicine maintains Images from the History of Medicine (**wwwihm.nlm.nih.gov/cgi-bin/gw_44_3/chameleon?skin=nlm&lng=en**).

Appendix B

Journals in the
Abridged Index Medicus
(AIM): Core Clinical Journals

THE *Abridged Index Medicus*, which the National Library of Medicine stopped printing in 1997, was designed for individual clinicians and the libraries of small hospitals and clinics. It contained bibliographic information on articles from more than a hundred English language journals. Although the printed version is a historical artifact, the AIM subset of journals is still being maintained as a means for limiting searches. In PubMed, this subset is also called "Core Clinical Journals." It can be useful in producing a quick—though incomplete—list of citations. While the AIM subset is not ideal, you may find it useful in setting up your own personal list of journals for searching.

Acad Med
> Academic Medicine: Journal of the Association of American
> Medical Colleges

AJR Am J Roentgenol
> AJR. American Journal of Roentgenology

Am Fam Physician
> American Family Physician

Am Heart J
> American Heart Journal

Am J Cardiol
> American Journal of Cardiology

Am J Clin Nutr
> American Journal of Clinical Nutrition

Am J Clin Pathol
  American Journal of Clinical Pathology

Am J Med
  American Journal of Medicine

Am J Med Sci
  American Journal of the Medical Sciences

Am J Nurs
  American Journal of Nursing

Am J Obstet Gynecol
  American Journal of Obstetrics and Gynecology

Am J Ophthalmol
  American Journal of Ophthalmology

Am J Pathol
  American Journal of Pathology

Am J Phys Med Rehabil
  American Journal of Physical Medicine and Rehabilitation

Am J Psychiatry
  American Journal of Psychiatry

Am J Public Health
  American Journal of Public Health

Am J Respir Crit Care Med
  American Journal of Respiratory and Critical Care Medicine

Am J Surg
  American Journal of Surgery

Am J Trop Med Hyg
  American Journal of Tropical Medicine and Hygiene

Anaesthesia
  Anaesthesia

Anesth Analg
  Anesthesia and Analgesia

Anesthesiology
  Anesthesiology

Ann Emerg Med
  Annals of Emergency Medicine

Ann Intern Med
> Annals of Internal Medicine

Ann Otol Rhinol Laryngol
> Annals of Otology, Rhinology and Laryngology

Ann Surg
> Annals of Surgery

Ann Thorac Surg
> Annals of Thoracic Surgery

Arch Dermatol
> Archives of Dermatology

Arch Dis Child
> Archives of Disease in Childhood

Arch Dis Child Fetal Neonatal Ed
> Archives of Disease in Childhood. Fetal and Neonatal Edition

Arch Environ Health
> Archives of Environmental Health

Arch Gen Psychiatry
> Archives of General Psychiatry

Arch Intern Med
> Archives of Internal Medicine

Arch Neurol
> Archives of Neurology

Arch Ophthalmol
> Archives of Ophthalmology

Arch Otolaryngol Head Neck Surg
> Archives of Otolaryngology — Head and Neck Surgery

Arch Pathol Lab Med
> Archives of Pathology and Laboratory Medicine

Arch Pediatr Adolesc Med
> Archives of Pediatrics and Adolescent Medicine

Arch Phys Med Rehabil
> Archives of Physical Medicine and Rehabilitation

Arch Surg
> Archives of Surgery

Arthritis Rheum
>Arthritis and Rheumatism

BJOG
>BJOG: An International Journal of Obstetrics and Gynaecogy
>[continues British Journal of Obstetrics and Gynaecology]

Blood
>Blood

BMJ
>BMJ (Clinical Research Ed.)
>[continues British Medical Journal]

Br J Radiol
>British Journal of Radiology

Br J Surg
>British Journal of Surgery

Brain
>Brain

CA Cancer J Clin
>CA: A Cancer Journal for Clinicians

Cancer
>Cancer

Chest
>Chest

Circulation
>Circulation

Clin Orthop
>Clinical Orthopaedics and Related Research

Clin Pediatr
>Clinical Pediatrics

Clin Pharmacol Ther
>Clinical Pharmacology and Therapeutics

CMAJ
>CMAJ
>[continues Canadian Medical Association Journal]

Crit Care Med
>Critical Care Medicine

Cur Probl Surg
>Current Problems in Surgery

Diabetes
>Diabetes

Dig Dis Sci
>Digestive Diseases and Sciences

Dis Mon
>Disease-A-Month

Endocrinology
>Endocrinology

Gastroenterology
>Gastroenterology

Geriatrics
>Geriatrics

Gut
>Gut

Heart
>Heart (British Cardiac Society)

Heart Lung
>Heart and Lung

Hosp Health Netw
>Hospitals and Health Networks / AHA

J Allergy Clin Immunol
>Journal of Allergy and Clinical Immunology

J Am Coll Cardiol
>Journal of the American College of Cardiology

J Am Coll Surg
>Journal of the American College of Surgeons

J Am Diet Assoc
> Journal of the American Dietetic Association

J Bone Joint Surg Am
> Journal of Bone and Joint Surgery. American Volume

J Bone Joint Surg Br
> Journal of Bone and Joint Surgery. British Volume

J Clin Endocrinol Metab
> Journal of Clinical Endocrinology and Metabolism

J Clin Invest
> Journal of Clinical Investigation

J Clin Pathol
> Journal of Clinical Pathology

J Fam Pract
> Journal of Family Practice

J Gerontol A Biol Sci Med Sci
> Journals of Gerontology. Series A, Biological Sciences and Medical Sciences

J Gerontol B Psychol Sci Soc Sci
> Journals of Gerontology. Series B, Psychological Sciences and Social Sciences

J Immunol
> Journal of Immunology

J Infect Dis
> Journal of Infectious Diseases

J Lab Clin Med
> Journal of Laboratory and Clinical Medicine

J Laryngol Otol
> Journal of Laryngology and Otology

J Nerv Ment Dis
> Journal of Nervous and Mental Disease

J Neurosurg
> Journal of Neurosurgery

J Nurs Adm
> Journal of Nursing Administration

J Oral Maxillofac Surg
        Journal of Oral and Maxillofacial Surgery

J Pediatr
        Journal of Pediatrics

J Thorac Cardiovasc Surg
        Journal of Thoracic and Cardiovascular Surgery

J Toxicol Clin Toxicol
        Journal of Toxicology. Clinical Toxicology

J Trauma
        Journal of Trauma

J Urol
        Journal of Urology

JAMA
        JAMA
        [continues Journal of the American Medical Association]

Lancet
        Lancet

Mayo Clin Proc
        Mayo Clinic Proceedings

Med Clin North Am
        Medical Clinics of North America

Med Lett Drugs Ther
        Medical Letter on Drugs and Therapeutics

Medicine
        Medicine; Analytical Reviews of General Medicine,
        Neurology, Psychiatry, Dermatology, and Pediatrics

N Engl J Med
        New England Journal of Medicine

Neurology
        Neurology

Nurs Clin North Am
        Nursing Clinics of North America
Nurs Outlook
        Nursing Outlook
Nurs Res
        Nursing Research

Obstet Gynecol
        Obstetrics and Gynecology
Orthop Clin North Am
        Orthopedic Clinics of North America

Pediatr Clin North Am
        Pediatric Clinics of North America
Pediatrics
        Pediatrics
Phys Ther
        Physical Therapy
Plast Reconstr Surg
        Plastic and Reconstructive Surgery
Postgrad Med
        Postgraduate Medicine
Prog Cardiovasc Dis
        Progress in Cardiovascular Diseases
Public Health Rep
        Public Health Reports

Radiol Clin North Am
        Radiologic Clinics of North America
Radiology
        Radiology
Rheumatology
        Rheumatology (Oxford, England)
        [continues British journal of Rheumatology]

South Med J
> Southern Medical Journal

Surg Clin North Am
> Surgical Clinics of North America

Surgery
> Surgery

Urol Clin North Am
> Urologic Clinics of North America

Index

A

AB, 25
Abbreviations for data elements
 or indexes, 22, 24–28
Abridged Index Medicus
 journals in, 111–119
 subset use of, 40, 111
Abstracts
 limitations of, 93–94
 sample of, 25
 text words in, 36–39
Accidents
 place in MeSH trees, 49–50
 use of MeSH for, 45–46,
 49–50
Accidents, traffic
 place in MeSH trees, 50
 telephones and, 45–46
 use of MeSH for, 45–46,
 49–50
Acquired immunodeficiency
 syndrome. *See also* AIDS
 first use of MeSH for, 53
 wide use of MeSH for, 89–90
Actual causes of death paper. *See*
 McGinnis & Foege paper
AD, 22, 26, 31
Address, 22, 26, 31
Adiposity
 text word use of, 24, 25, 30,
 34, 35, 36, 37
Administration & dosage subheading, 57
Adolescent
 use of MeSH for, 66
Adrenergic antagonists

use of MeSH for, 59
Adrenergic beta-antagonists
 hypertension and, 59
 use of MeSH for, 59
Adult
 use of MeSH for, 66
Adverse effects subheading, 57
 aspirin and, 54–55
Affiliation index
 abbreviation for, 22
 sample display of, 26
 use of, 31
African Americans
 use of MeSH for, 90
Age groups, 65–66
Aged
 hypertension and, 90
 use of MeSH for, 66
Aged, 80 and over
 use of MeSH for, 66
Agency for Healthcare Research
 and Quality, 107, 109
Agonists subheading, 57
AHRQ, 107, 109
AIDS. *See also* Acquired immunodeficiency syndrome
 subject subset, 41, 100
AIM
 journals in, 111–119
 sample display with, 27
 subset use of, 40, 111
Air pollution
 use of MeSH for, 91–92
Alcohol drinking
 breast neoplasms and, 80,
 81–82
 use of MeSH for, 80, 81

Aleve, 52
ALLHAT trial, 39
ALTBIB, 41
American Diabetes Association, 74
American Heart Journal
  on-line for subscribers, 94
  part of AIM, 111
American Journal of Health-System Pharmacy
  on-line for subscribers, 94
American Journal of Public Health
  obesity reviews in, 78–79
  on-line for subscribers, 94
  part of AIM, 112
Analogs & derivatives subheading, 57
Analysis subheading, 57
Analytical, diagnostic and therapeutic techniques and equipment category, 47
Anatomy category, 47, 49
AND
  definition of, 7
  graphic display of, 9
  limiting to humans with, 9
  table illustration of, 8
Angina-related MeSH
  explosions of, 51–52
  MeSH trees, 50–51
Angiotensin-converting enzyme inhibitors
  use of MeSH for, 59
Animal
  Boolean strategies and, 9
  testing alternatives, 41
Animal diseases
  use of MeSH for, 58
Annals of Internal Medicine
  on-line for subscribers, 94
  part of AIM, 113

Answering services
  use of MeSH for, 53
Antagonists & inhibitors subheading, 57
Anthropology, education, sociology and social phenomena category, 47
Anti-allergic agents
  use of MeSH for, 60
Anti-infective agents
  use of MeSH for, 60
Anti-inflammatory agents
  use of MeSH for, 60
Anti-inflammatory agents, nonsteroidal
  pharmacological action of, 62
  use of MeSH for, 62, 65
Antihypertensive agents. *See also* Hypertension
  place in MeSH trees, 59
  use of MeSH for, 53, 59
Antilipemic agents
  use of MeSH for, 60
Antineoplastic agents
  use of MeSH for, 60
Antirheumatic agents,
  use of MeSH for, 60
Arm
  place in MeSH trees, 49
Aspirin
  adverse effects from, 54–55
  anti-inflammatory effects of, 62
  antiplatelet effects of, 62
  cardioprotective effects of, 65
  GI bleeding from, 54
  history of, 55–56
  osteoarthritis and, 8
  other MeSH and, 8
  pharmacokinetics of, 55
  pharmacological action of,

E

Economics subheading, 56, 57
  aspirin and, 55
EDAT, 28
Editorial
  excerpt from, 81–82
  publication type, 75, 81–82
Elbow
  place in MeSH trees, 49
Elder abuse
  use of MeSH for, 66
Elderly. *See* Aged
EMBASE, 108–109
Embryology subheading, 56
EndNote, 29, 96
Entrez. *See also* PubMed,
    PubMed Central, Bookshelf,
    etc.
  databases in, 95, 99, 105
  history of, 14–15
  journals database, 33, 103,
    104–105
  MeSH database, 52, 54,
    55, 58, 61, 62, 66, 67, 100,
    101–102, 109
Environment and public health
  place in MeSH trees, 49
Environmental pollution
  use of MeSH for, 91
Enzymology subheading, 56
Epidemiology
  editorial from, 81–82
Epidemiology subheading, 56
Epistaxis
  use of MeSH for, 38–39
Estrogen replacement therapy
  use of MeSH for, 92
Ethnology subheading, 56
Etiology subheading, 56
Evaluation of search results, 23,

33–34, 37–39, 90, 92–93, 95
Evidence-based medicine
  in PubMed, 41
  use of MeSH for, 76, 80
  Web-based resources for, 107,
    109, 110
Exercise. *See also* Physical activity
  use of MeSH for, 27, 34–35
Explosions of MeSH, 51–52, 53
Extremities
  place in MeSH trees, 49

F

Falls. *See* Accidents
FDA. *See* Food and Drug Admin-
    istration
Fever
  ibuprofen and, 6
  other MeSH and, 8
Fields. *See* Indexes
Fingers
  place in MeSH trees, 48–49
  use of MeSH for, 49
Foege, WH
  classic paper by, 32
Food and Drug Administration
  phases of clinical trials for, 77
  Web address for, 109
Forearm
  place in MeSH trees, 49
Formularies
  use of MeSH for, 58
Frail elderly
  use of MeSH for, 66

G

Gastrointestinal agents
  use of MeSH for, 60
Gastrointestinal hemorrhage

HTML. *See* World wide web
Hu, Frank B, 24, 26, 29–30
HUGO, 13
Humantities category, 47
Humans
limiting searches to, 9
Hydroxymethylglutaryl-CoA
reductase inhibitors
mapped from "statins," 52, 62
use of pharmacological action
for, 62–64
use of MeSH for, 52, 62–64
Hypertension. *See also* Antihypertensive agents
Chicago and, 66
compliance among African
Americans with, 90
drug therapy for elderly, 90
mapping from "high blood
pressure," 52
practice guideline for, 74
related MeSH, 53
use of MeSH for, 53, 59, 74,
76, 89, 90
Hypertension
practice guideline in, 74
Hypokalemia
use of MeSH for, 9

I

IBM, 5
IBM cards. *See* Punch cards
Ibuprofen
drug interactions and, 6, 65
fever and, 6
kidney failure, acute and, 6
osteoarthritis and, 6–8
other MeSH and, 8
review articles and, 65
use of MeSH for, 6–8, 65

ICD-9-CM_2005, 13
ICD-10, 13
Images on the Web, 110
Immunology subheading,
56, 57
*Index Catalogue of the Library of
the Surgeon General's Office*
history of, 3–4
Web address for, 105
Index Medicus
history of, 4–16
Major MeSH index like, 64
Indexes. *See also* specific indexes
(Medical subject headings,
etc.)
abbreviations for, 22
definition of, 21
frequently used, table of, 22
sample citation display of,
24–28
Indexing, history of, 3–16
Infant
use of MeSH for, 65
Infant, newborn
use of MeSH for, 65
Infant nutrition
use of MeSH for, 66
Information science
category, 46, 47, 68
use of MeSH for, 68
Information services
use of MeSH for, 68
Information storage and retrieval
use of MeSH for, 12, 16
Infotrieve, 101
In-process citations. *See* PubMed
Interactions, 38
Isolation & purification subheading, 57

Precision vs. recall, 33–34, 37–39

Prevention & control subheading, 56
breast neoplasms and, 71

Pro-Cite, 29

Professional associations on Web, 110

Protease inhibitors
use of MeSH for, 59

Proteins
supplementary concepts for, 48, 61

Psychiatry and psychology category, 47

Psychology subheading, 56

PT, 22, 26, 40

PubChem, 102

Public health
American journal of, 79, 94, 112
Billings's interest in, 5
Harvard school of, 26
images, 110
place in MeSH trees, 49
San Francisco Dept of, 31, 45
U.S. Gov't role in, 109
Web sites, 109–110

Public Library of Science, 104

Publication date, 31–32

Publication Type
frequently used, list of 75
sample display of, 26
MeSH category, 47
uses of, 40, 73–82

PubMed. *See also* Medical Subject Headings; MEDLINE
clinical queries page, 41, 81, 100
compared to MEDLINE, viii, 21, 32, 100

date citation added to, 28, 32
details tab, 23, 67, 100
filters in, 41, 81
history of, 13–16
in-process citations, 29, 103
interface to MEDLINE, 1, 13–16, 99–100
limits in, 40, 41, 73, 100
PMIDs in, 22, 24, 28–29, 96
related articles in, 14, 39, 91
single citation matcher, 30
special queries page, 41, 81, 100
subject subsets, 41
systematic reviews in, 41, 107
truncation in, 38
tutorial, 12, 101–102
unique identifier, 22, 24, 28–29
Web address for, 99

PubMed Central
DTD for, 15
full-text articles in, 14, 94, 104
limit PubMed search to, 40

Punch cards, 4–10
computer memory like, 6

Q

Qualifiers. *See* subheadings
Questions
ask right ones, 89, 90, 91–92

R

Radiation effects subheading, 57
Radiography subheading, 56
Radionuclide imaging subheading, 56
Radiotherapy subheading, 56